Contemporary Fireside Poems

An Anthology

Edited by

Fatou Taqi

&

Philip Foday Yamba Thulla

Sierra Leonean Writers Series

Contemporary Fireside Poems

ISBN: 978-99910-54-62-9

Sierra Leonean Writers Series

CONTENTS

i

This book is dedicated to all members of the

Salone Writers Social Media Forum

Preface

When the idea of a social media-sourced anthology was first proposed, it sounded hilarious to many, especially so when two seemingly inexperienced editors for it were similarly proposed, not knowing it could be a futuristic alternative to the 'fireside gathering' that was popular then. There was this frequently asked question among anthropologists: Does conversation change when people sit around a fire? The consensus was that, yes, it does change. Deborah Netburn (2016) states that there is value "in sitting around a campfire, listening to stories, singing songs and letting yourself stare mesmerized into the flickering flames…". This is not just a traditional African custom, but a typical Sierra Leonean avenue of 'edu-tainment', where cultures, mores and traditions were passed down by the elders, morals and lessons taught, whilst providing entertainment for the evenings before bedtime. Besides the entrenched belief that people are much more open when they sit around a fire, the expressed view, however, is that these public gatherings are no longer clearly visible among communities the world over. The communal medium has been eroded by the Internet or specifically, substituted by affordances that have closely paralleled the ancient fire side gathering. The composition of this anthology, *Contemporary Fireside Poems,* is a manifestation of this dynamism and we are pleased to offer you this alternative. Poems published in this anthology share a common standard: writers sharing their thoughts via the *Salone Writers social media forum*, pieces critiqued before being considered for submissions. In this way, social harmony and equality are promoted both with Sierra Leoneans in the diaspora and those at home. In a sense, the campfire story-telling and 'riddling' sessions are not altogether lost, and as Weissner notes, has bonded the critics and writers (on the *SWF*); helped them in telling social information and in entertaining and sharing emotions.

This anthology provides a fine mixture of writers, subjects and themes—there are 'old', expert, veteran voices as well as 'new', budding voices. During the process of editing the various contributions, it was decided at some point to divide the publication into two parts. One that focused on poetry and the other that focused on short stories. *Contemporary Fireside Poems* is the first part of the collection.

The truth is, the anthology creates the space for a true and unique Sierra Leonean style of creativity, where spontaneity is not compromised.

In conclusion, we would like to express our gratitude to:

Mallam Osman Sankoh (Prof.) of the *Sierra Leonean Writers Series* and Director, INDEPTH for proposing this brilliant idea of using the *Salone Writers Social Media Forum* as the source for the collection of this anthology and for suggesting us as editors of the anthology; Gbanabom Hallowell for initiating the forum and bringing together Sierra Leoneans around the world who have a passion for the creative arts; and all members of the forum for their criticisms and recommendations. You are all highly appreciated.

FT & PFYT

Poems

Conteh, Samuella Julia

Introduction to Poem, "Something the Lord Made"

This poem is not the product of a vain imagination…
This poem is an appreciation of God's handiwork.
This poem was not borne of carnality…
This poem is a realization of who I am.
This poem was not written to thrill or to impress…
This poem is a confirmation that I was never a mistake.

When God created the world and all therein,
He said 'Let there be'…and there was! That would sound like conjuring.
When he made 'man', He first carved him out of clay, breathed into his nostrils to give him life.

Then God decided the earth needed a fairer being, so He sent man off; into a beautiful sleep, removed one of his ribs…and He made woman…ME!
So, I am 'Something the Lord Made', and that is the motif of this poem!

Something the Lord Made

The Lord made me a WONDER.
And that which He made so,
Can never be bound.
For like an eagle,
Even the stillness of the wind
Can never hinder my flight.
I am something the Lord made.

The Lord gave me a SPARKLE
And that which He so gave,
Needs not the sun to shine.
For like a firefly,
Even the bleakest of nights
Can never darken my path.
I am something the Lord made.

The Lord made me a JEWEL
And that which He so designed,
 Would stand the test of time.
For even the longest haul in the mud
Can never hide my glint.
I am something the Lord made.

I am coming out of my cocoon
And if I refuse to break open
Someone, something, or any force,
With grace or without, would do it.
Then the world would know me;
I am something the Lord made.

Groans and Moans

Groans bring thoughts of a goat
In pain!
From a bruised member
In Anguish,
From pains in groins,
From a member stuck in a thicket,
In the height of readiness,
In the absence of a wanton vulva,
To empty the seeds of his soul.

Moans bring thoughts of a man
Of his oomph!
To the splendour of his manhood,
In readiness to jam his member,
In a garden of joy.
Sleekness and ticklish,
Gasping for more
In orgasmic delights;
Reaching for heights,
In total abandonment.

The Writer Never Left

The Writer Never Left;
He lived in a world all for his own:
Some days his eyes flew wild,
Even showing bloodied pain
Or smart the hood of shame.
For in his own world,
There was bloodiness everywhere
He ought to save and be safe,
He and his colleagues saw the carnage.
So, though he never left home,
He was never home with his beloved.

For the writer in him took over the man in him
And he forgot to romance his beloved
But let his mind to wander the Asian deserts,
Searching for the enemy searching for him.
He equaled his colleagues
In strength and passion,
Leaving none for his beloved;
His mind exhausted in yonder lands.
So, though he never left home,
He was never home with his beloved.

The writer in him raced with comrades
And wrote on the pages of the soil;
As equals in voices and desires,
So trekked oh! How he trekked
In the Australasia depths,
But he forgot the depth of his passion,
So while he roamed the lands of his mind,
Another roamed the luxury of his lady,
For though he never left home,
He was never home with his beloved.

Goodbye My Aborted Foetus

Yes
You are a part and half of me:
The half that said no;
The unwilling part,
The half that cried
A cry not of ecstasy;
The part that remained unfulfilled,
Except that with pain.

Yes
You are a part and half of him:
The half that forced
The part that scourged;
The half that was a complete demon
With a wicked gleam in his evil eyes,
The part that remained deaf to its pleas,
Except that they urged him on.

No
I desire not an image of him,
So what if you turn out like him?
You my sliced foetus
Would be my second death,
For you would rape my joy
As your father raped my dignity,
Except that I would rather not.

Why Should I Have to Look Like You

Why should I have to look like you,
Speak like you,
Live where you live?
To see my humanity,
I am who I want to be,
Where I want to be,
With whom I want to be,
As guarded by an impartial law.

I don't want my rights only on paper,
In briefcases for table talks.
I want my rights right here and now!

I don't have to love like you do
Or hate as you hate;
Or believe what you believe
For you to unshackle my humanity
From your subtle discrimination,
Chaining my mind in subjection,
I want to be me and only me,
As unique as I was meant to be.

I don't want my rights only on paper,
In briefcases for table talks.
I want my rights right here and now!

Den se wi nor sabi buk,
Bot wi no we wi ed de at.
Den se wi nor get pawa,
Bot wi no we wi at den ful.
Den se wi na pekin dem,
Bot wi no we den de mas wi fut.
Den se wi nor undastand natin,

Bot wi no se i du so.
Den tink se wi na bikful dem,
Bot wi no se wi nor de gri egen.

Woman, Reinvent Thyself!

I refuse to play the victim,
Just because I was born with a rose
For like my brother,
I am endowed with a brain and a mind

I refuse to be violated by dirt,
For my father's debts
Or my mother's vain whims
Or to keep my brother in school

I refuse to play the victim,
For like my male counterpart,
I will use my brain and not my diadem
To pass my class and move ahead;
My bubbly boobs in my bra shall stay.
So speak to my face where there's a mouth.

I refuse to be lulled by taunting favours;
A display of false fragility
Or weakness of supposed male superiority
Just because it is said to be.

My sister would stop playing the victim;
And see there's servitude in being kept,
If you are happy being called after a cat,
Remember that they have not just furs;
They sure have claws too.
To have a rose, a fluffy wreath of leaves, make you not a
cat.

Stop making excuses where there are none!
Choose a better option for a better lot,
Source courage from others

Who chose to make it right.
Woman, a rose is a tiny prickle
Of a whole wonderful shrub.
So don't overshadow your strength;
Make you vulnerable; a charity case.

'No rose, no thorns'!
So stand up for what you are,
Displaying sobriety, not sexuality.

If your worth's about your rose,
Scream 'til someone listens;
Speak 'til someone does you right;
See that you are made human too.

Fofanah, Kemurl Mustapha Abdul

The Writer's Coming Home

The writer's coming home
To embrace his beloved
After the long battle in Euro's chest,
Rattling with comrades,
Pens of the soil,
Equals in size and weights,
The writer's coming home.

The writer's coming home
To romance his beloved
After the stretching search in the Asian deserts,
Wrestling with comrades,
Inks of the soil,
Equals in strength and passion,
The writer's coming home.

The writer's coming home
To wander with his beloved
After the exhaustions compete
In the Americas;
Racing with comrades,
Pages of the soil,
Equals in voices and desires,
The writer's coming home.

The writer's coming home
To rest with his beloved
After the trekking expeditions
In the Australasia depth,
Roaming with comrades,
Pens of the soils,
Equals in love and worries,

The writer's coming home.

The writer's come home
To sell, to live, with his beloved
After the bitter experiences by the skin of Africa's teeth,
Dancing with comrades,
Sons of the soil,
Equals in minds and thoughts,
The writer's sailing home to his own soil, to meet his beloved.

Melodies from Home

My heart in exile
Bears this broken chord
That echoes your pain.
It mimics the rhythm of your fragile scale
That beats my thoughts.
As we move in droves,
I hear your nightingales,
Your canaries,
Your roars,
Your hisses;
I hear the bawls.
As militia ravaged their nests,
I hear the rush
From thousands Kalashnikovs,
As they compose eulogies
from dying voices,
I hear the waves from your urban-huts;
Its crooked drum-beats
Romance my soul with wistful tunes.

I pause,
In the heart of this foreign road
To gaze at your bloodless veins.
In my mind's eye,
Your face wore this cracked smile.
I saw your women,
Your children,
Your adults,
Your youth,
Searching for themselves
In the mouth of death;
Barely escaping its decisive touch,

I saw them crossing your deserts, your pools
With disheveled bodies,
Trying to reach my battered hands.
They did not know how broken my spirit stood
Between these strange walls,
Bemoaning the painful melodies,
Exuding from my distorted home.

Fortunate Pupils from Africa's Village

Down the steep lane, we sauntered, marathon-like, every day to classes.
We rode bare-feet on pitches, dressed in rocks and steel grasses.
With our uniforms tinged, oozing strong masculine sweat from inner arms,
We hymned the songs of school tasks and working on insatiable stretch of low flat farm lands.
Our schools, an isle of open air, moved by seasons and weathers,
Our class rooms, the ruins of nothing, built by nature's tendering feather,
Our books, rough sheets, slates and tree trunks, flattened by knives and painted like our skins,
Our chairs and desks, our legs, our brothers back, the earth, our cloths made clean;
No anthem for us or melancholic strings to take as a school song,
But every day, we chanted praises to Him above, with boastful lips and silent tongues,
Each class, we closed when the Maker's torch blinded our eyes,
Each year, we dwelled, no sport, no dance, no excitement, to steer our infant emotions,
Our teachers, like prophets, preaching good-wills, with no hope for earthly rewards.
Is there any one, somewhere in this big blue bowl, with a grain of courage?
Please come forward.
We were the fortunate pupils of many Africa's villages:
We had no luxuries, but were happy to compose these few words from our Brain pages and carved out our
Strange scenes.

Demonic Verses

Demonic verses
Stem from their minds,
Written on broken plaques,
Recited to meager ears,
Embraced by dead souls.

Demonic verses
Crawl in their thoughts,
Written on battered books,
Taught in the open air,
Learned by dead souls

Demonic verses
Run in their veins,
Written on human skins,
Preached in "Godly" places,
Memorized by dead souls.

Demonic verses
Are Scriptures in their lips,
Coated with dead promises,
Anthems of self-gains,
Hymned by dead souls.

A Date with Satisfaction

I wish you could feel the sudden rush of fulfillment,
When you had a day out with satisfaction,
You would sit on the edge of Ganges, Euphrates and Tigris, in
one night
With your extracted ribs, lying beside you,
She snored melodies from Eden,
Whilst shades of vine chased the sun-brutes away.
You closed your eyes,
And pictured her soft lips smooching yours,
With Malombo in the center, gently blessing the bond.
You battled her in bliss,
Her body, an amour,
Built from steels of amber and Dusk,
Her hair, a helmet of silk, swift and gallant,
Her eyes, a pair of binoculars that spotted her heart beating
within yours,
Her nose, sensitive to the waves and fragrance of tender touch.
Lovers so tensely ready for dwell
Like a thousand Achilles in charging motion.
Despite her defense,
You slit her,
Muscular attachments pierced her ovum,
Seeding your genes.
You watched her stomach rise
And detonate; killing you both with love.

Dead Man Story

Dead man walking,
Dead man trekking in droves,
Dead man chasing nothing,
Dead man is like a mad captain
Searching for a pin in the Mediterranean wide:
He passes by the ocean's graves,
He passes dumb, deaf and blind,
He marathons cities of the ocean;
He marathons aimlessly.

Dead man rides,
Dead man moves in droves,
Dead man runs for nothing,
Dead man is like a mad captain
Searching for stars beneath the sun's breast:
He passes by graves of dead ashes,
He passes deaf, dumb and blind,
He flies the cities in firmament;
He flies selfishly.

Dead man is alive,
Dead man lives in droves,
Dead man lives for nothing,
Dead man is like a mad captain
Searching for his wants, forgetting his needs:
He passes by dozens of dead men,
He passes deaf, dumb and blind,
He builds hundreds of fortune,
He builds them pointlessly;
For a dead man takes nothing to the grave.

The Sudden Death of a Writer's Skill

Waking up one dreadful morning,
Emptiness ransacking you,
No verses left to recite,
Ink, dried; pen, barren,
The mind could not grip its thoughts,
Stories floating about,
Skills had divorced you;
You are drowning,
You can't catch the sail,
You gasp for life,
Resuscitating colleagues
But your lifeline is amiss,
For your talents are gone;
Nothing to feed from,
Even your eyes keep blinking,
And your senses reject to spell,
You wail in distress,
You pretend,
But nothing done,
You are a dead writer!
You died suddenly!

I Will One Day Be Free

You may tie me to your will,
You may beat me with your steel,
You may cheat me by your use of crooked skill,
You may taunt me as you feel,

You cannot take away my rights above
You cannot take away my love for a dove,
For I'll one day be free; free to look the way I love,
Free to believe or not, free to fashion my body curves.

You may seize my inherited might,
You may deny my eyes the bliss of nature's light,
You may turn all my days into dreadful night,
You may rally my village against my rights,

You cannot take away my smiles,
You cannot wrap my freedom with your lies,
For I'll one day be free; free to bathe in the great Nile,
Free to survive, free to chase all!
 I resist; you, I deny!

French, Miatta

My Reflections on 6th January

Epiphany:
That morning, as quoted, they came from the East.
In many churches this date is still a feast.
But then these men were more than three,
They could not be the Magi who came, the Lord to see,
And so with the final strains of "Noel, Noel..."
They started a stanza of living hell.
And just as was promised to you and me,
They opened the jails' gates and set prisoners free.
Instead of singing "Gloria in Excelsis",
Our refrain was "Miserére nobis".

Hallowell, Gbanabom

When Should New Dates Ask For Money

When the date is old
And I have drunk
My soup and beers too,
When her tongue
Loosens to show a vein,
When the teeth remain
White and befriend
Her bloody tongue
On a daily basis,
When the clothes she
Wears keep their perfumes,
When the dollar
Rises below her eyes
And when the banks
And all their ATMs
Are on strike.

An Ode to a Brand New Kiss

Drunk in my virtual being,
I have been kissed
With the lips of blade
And my two worlds
Of life and death
Breathe impatiently
To own this mortal lips.

Let the night that built
Me perish in the day,
For no time shall furl
Around this romantic
Coat of mine. The sea
Is black, mirroring my skin.

My teeth went to sleep
Shedding their steel.
I will celebrate on
The campus of Yamba
And wait for another
Day a new Celia will
Rise from the dust!

Of Moaning and Groaning

And then the adrenaline
Conquered my brain.
It was already falling off
February 14 and nobody
Had died in the beleaguered
House, but I moaned the flesh
The woman groaned through
The dutiful nose.

The wind twisted
And fell on the dark bodies.
Two souls perished
Under the weights
Of the bodies of night.
The power of the pipe liquid
Is In the throat of a dry dam.

It rained and the wretched
Souls suffered a heart attack
Through the lavender buds.
New modes of moaning
Tell themselves in cries
And a victim is heard baying.

Tonight I have drunk
Like Adam seeking
To know why I am
Without a dress of leaves
And why Eve is no
Longer Eve and why my
Brother Farouk does not look
So well in the beer bar any more than does Mallam!

Confessions of an Aged Poet

My left eye gorged in love,
The bottle of hope
Broke on my uneleventh
Hour and a godless rain
Fell on my only flour.
I baked my love instead,
I cried over my loafless love.

My right eye gorged,
I felt the window
Of love rattling in the wind
After my brothers had
Harvested their pies.

I am here waiting for that
Female poet who forgot
To love me in her prime!

I Would Have Been a Damned Good Lawyer

I would have read
Kant and swallowed
His ethics,

Passed by the fire
Walking my shadow
Through its theory,

Measured the sand
In the heart of the desert
And dug an oasis,

Defeated the prosecutor
And healed the defender,
Cooked him whole in pot,

Read the Bible in its
Tablet format
And the Quran in Kaaba,

Sent the magistrate
A flower and the judge
Should have bowed
Before my poetry.

I Love You between Your Eyes

in the end, my love,
the day shall walk
Away, with its bright
eyes sticking into mud
and in the blistering
night, I shall love you
between your naked eyes.

fascist thinkers, let
me into your theory,
for I am full of love,
and of the full pint
of oil. Siddhartha, tease
me with your left
because my right hand
cannot hold a flower.

I am the finger clue
coming against deserts,
against stagnant Niles
smelling of orchids
and of the life of dead
things raging in their own
Sea. I stand beside

Myself, half a thought,
looking like a god, no
longer able to stop
the world from showing
love while killing every
breath.

fuck to that sweet rose,
that tired muscles
of the wretched sea
and the darkness of the
careless mountain.

fuck to my bread,
close to the plate,
the little finger kissing
itself in the lips, the knife
lying on the table
after cutting its own
bread into two halves.

fuck to my pain mixing
with unpardonable tears,
wetting my face each
time a love drinks
the hemlock.

speaking of which,
fuck to Pushkin for
loving too much
with the taste of flower
in his rabid mouth
and a worthless sword
below his other belt.

just before I say fuck
to you, I must rip off your
blatant eyes for ease
of the literary pain
you are condemned into.

So fuck to you!

The Trial of an Aborted Child

Night-mid creatures
Pause in foetus
Dame of earth
Crawl and not talk
Pink death
Sad sorrow steam
Spoilt of the earth
Apple tree people
Naked foetus
All mankind
Born or aborted
Knife world
Kingdom divided
Blood doctors
Doctored blood
Flesh of dust
Killing cry
Dust to dust
Mama weeps
Tenured criminals
Bring forth
Chameleon babies
Umbilical abscesses
Man hurt woman
Baby built on
Life support
The image of (wo)man
God aborted
Bruised apples
Falling bruised
Earth wind fire
Sorrow people

Killing census
Bathing money-child
Weep weep weep.

Born Aborted

You killed the flesh
Poured my blood
But I came forth

You gnashed your
Teeth crushing me
Between your fingers
And yet I came forth

You panted in hate
Murdering me in
Cold blood against
My hurting you
And yet I came forth

You ripped me apart
Because you were raped
A crime I didn't commit
And still I came forth

I came dead yet I came
My name is not rape
My soul is tabula rasa
Mama, I am not guilty

You deprived me of a name.

I am in the shade

Of a tree because
A man is standing
On my left toe.
I am bathing in sand
Because the sea
Is on strike;
Yesterday I went out
Without my heart,
Searching for a vacant
Woman;
I laughed to the miner
Who had drunk
His tongue down
His own pit.
The face of two
Did not save his tears
So I decided to cry
With him, even
Shedding a sweat
Where his dried up
Quickly.
After all my pursuit
For a woman and
My sadness for
The miner, I put
On a resolved face
To return him and wear
My heart to come
Out again.

I am Sacred Tonight

The man bit my flesh
For a little truth.
I am a miner, and
I have the hunger
Of greed. Working
For the driver whose
Train runs on my back.
A man is approaching
Me with gold
In his stomach.
I am the overseer
Who must tell
The boss that a fellow
Is in his fetish
Tonight and that
Must be killed with
A knife.
Yet I have my own
Sorrow limping
In my stomach.
My friend told me
To digest it, but
I do not have
The intestine for that.
Tonight I feel the rain
Whispering in my
Stomach with a whole
World turning
Into its own planet.
Give me free!

Ever since

I was informed
That any poem sent
Here will be published,
I have learned to climb
Forest trees,
To eat my apples
In the dark,
To settle for simple
Music,
To cater for my own
Sentiments,
To live like a broken
Plate with water Trickling below
Its temperature.
I am particularly
Lost in my little fear
That the whisper
I am familiar with
No longer can
Maintain a secret.
There is a thread
Leading to my being
Put out of this forum
No longer sounds
Like the poem
My father read to me
Before my birth.
I am moving waters
From the bottom
Of rivers after clearing
Them of their slavish
Warmth.
I stand corrected

If I have become
A quick judge
In the face
Of a drunken
Magistrate;
But I have to defend
Myself every drop
Of my blood!

Poem for the Last Moment of Poetry

In the event
That the world comes
To an end March 6
2016, I want to climb
The Alps in my sleep;
I want to be the last
American president
In Dubai holding
The code of the atomic
Bomb and right after
Entering it I forget
How to stop it from
Annihilating mankind.
I want to be the last
Man seeing the chards
Of the once gigantic
Earth with the sun
And the moon detaching
Themselves from
The palavers of the world.
Then, at that material
Moment, I suddenly
Remember the code
To avoid the nuclear bomb
From firing off.
Too late.
I shall turn to Putin
And say: fuck me
And fuck you too
For not listening
To Hilary Clinton.

Ibrahim, Zakiyyah Thara

When I Return

When I return home,
Pour me a tall, cold glass of ginger beer,
No, not ginger ale, spicy, carbonated,
Give me natural and earthy
Hot and cold, in my mouth,
Like the winds in December.

And when I leave there,
Get me a bowl of fruit –
Mangoes, paw-paws, baboon wine.
Let the juice run down my lips,
The same way the tears and make-up
Used to run,
After long days with high heels and low standards.

When I return,
Sit me outside in a lappa made by my people.
Let the breeze from the trees free me;
Inside, outside, wherever, in-between.
Don't let those cold winds touch me again.

When I stay,
Make a pot full of soup
And a plate of heavy pounded yam,
Let me eat with my hands.
I am at home, am I not?
Let me savor it; don't guilt- trip me
Or tell me to hurry up,
Or bombard me with: 'how unhealthy it is',
'How much calories',
'How much meat that's in it',
I don't care,

I haven't really eaten in a while.

And finally,
When I'm home again,
Sit me by the moon
While the birds fly home
And the chickens cockle-dooo no more.
Let the moon tell me how much it's missed me
As we talk under a forever sky
About a familiar place called home.

Aisha Died

Aisha died,
Holding my hand,
A ghostly smile on her pale face;
Her hollow face,
While my tears flowed
Onto the arm I held like a talisman.
But, the roof failed to protect us
From the torrential rain,
Zinc opened as a fisherman's net.
But, the drops sympathized with us
And so did the whole village.
Mama collapsed,
Papa acted a man; brave face,
But even I could see
The unshed tears
In his hollow eyes
As he had run all the way home,
When he heard the villagers' cry,
The hoe still in his hand,
The dirt still on him,
Clinging like second skin,
But I am happy,
Aisha died so young,
Still pure,
Innocent,
Because I would not have been able
To endure,
Her pain, would have,
Killed us softly,
So I wipe my tears,
I'm happy it is now,
Because she cannot feel the pain

And she can go live with the Angels
We read about in Sunday books,
In our memory she'll remain.

Jones, Harriet Yeanoh

Poverty

Who gave you such a horrible face
That terrifies every man you embrace?
Oh dreaded foe of the human race;
Man perpetually battles to avoid your disgrace.

You bring conflict into communities
When you inflict your terrible disease;
You leave folks homeless in cold to freeze
Their frail frames withstand not your violent breeze.

Fine men compromise their integrity
Day by day you lead them to iniquity;
Young girls no longer maintain their virginity
They cannot but relinquish their dignity.

Poverty! Are you a man or a woman?
For certainly you lack the grace of a swan.
Your degree of ferocity none fully can discern.
Beware! On your operations shall I impose a ban.

I swear you will not pursue me to the grave;
I am ready to fight with a heart strong and brave,
Fed up am I of being your slave,
Therefore have I come out of my cave.

Who gave you such a horrible face
That terrifies every man you embrace?
Oh dreaded foe of the human race;
That man perpetually battles to avoid your disgrace.

The Child's Plea

I am who you once were;
Be friendly and treat me with utmost care.
Do ensure my back's never bare;
On my own nothing can I afford to wear.

You're who I shall become;
Bring me up in a home loving and warm.
Care giving is a duty not only for mums;
Help protect me from society's worms.

I need love, care and protection;
My future depends on your decision.
'T may build or break national cohesion;
Endeavour to give me just education.

I need food, shelter and security;
And such to promote health and vitality.
Teach me love, truth and integrity;
Thus can we have a peaceful, stable society.

Kaifala, Francis Ben

My Phenomenal Woman

Nine months in her womb like a moving chain,
Hours endured of contraction pain,
Years of touching care- come shine or rain,
My Mother's love so true and plain.

Even in war and strife beyond mundane,
Remained steadfast on heights I should attain,
With Dad gone before my take on boyish gain,
Her shoulders my towering view of life's terrain.

Now with a worn but still lovely frame,
A victim of toil and hope; not self-acclaim,
Time is nigh for her reward to claim;
Pray death her life not its sooner aim.

With burning love like an Olympic flame,
Played her motherly role with no cry or blame.
She Watch'd me battle with a World to claim,
In silent prayer for a life of fame!

With no Dad beyond Nine to emulate,
Saw me through to become a lawyer to date;
With a purse too humble to ever inflate,
Led me to Masters in London's gates!

If God could grant wishes again and again,
He'll keep from her Death Angel's disdain
While the World joins me sing in refrain:
Phenomenal! Phenomenal! Madam Tewa Kaifala.

When Wells Run Dry

No door's so wide that can't be locked,
No light's so bright that can't be blocked,
No lightening flash without thunder bolt,
No burst of smoke without fire so close.
Where will we be when our wells run dry?

Nature's kind is bound to cease,
Flow of Wealth is sure to freeze.
So when we pluck our garden seeds,
'Tis wise to think that harvests ease
Like Joseph did in Egypt's days of need,

That's what should be in lands of care;
The leaders think on what is fair,
So guide their steps in strides of fear.
On rainy days do keep in careful ware,
What all would reap when seasons dare.

I look with awe as our futures wear;
Our leaders gladly sign what they ought to tear.
Like smoke in wind, our wealth disappear.
Educated fools indeed they are
Who read and write but can't infer.

With all their talks and smartly looks,
Colourful CV's and boastful title hooks,
They're moved around by foreign crooks
Who barely learnt to read their nursery books
But allowed to cart away our precious goods.

Doesn't State House know that wells dry out?
Hasn't Gloucester Street heard of Sovereign Fund Account?
Isn't George Street aware how called-in Bonds can wreck our

heights?
And keep our Cake in stock on pouring nights?
That children unborn can have their share of bites?

'Tis not too late to build our Rome!
For our hills and swamps their yield to keep,
Prepare for when Kono's saggy breasts no longer feed
And Foreign Foes with joy their homes recede,
But common sense is all we need!

Why should they Care?

Why do we think they'll really care?
With all they've fleec'd and made disappear?
They live like Kings and choke on lots of beer,
While families struggle for what to eat or share.

Their Children cruise to private schools;
They party and bathe in swimming pools.
In their corrupt eyes we're all nagging fools
They can use and dump like used-up tools.

But elections are soon to come,
Thinking we'll join their campaigns for some rum;
That's our time to treat 'em all like scum,
Sweep them with our votes like the hurricane storm.

'Tis our time to make our leaders 'ware
We're not all the fools they think we are.
Let all unite and speak with no fear!
Only our united voice can make our society fair.

Mandela's Way

Let peace in Africa reign;
Let it pour on us like the torrential rain
That in rainy days waters our terrain.
Let Africa, its peace maintain,
That war and strife may ne'er reign again,

Like the Trade wind that travels from the north to the west.
Let Madiba's spirit bring our people rest;
From the Gulf of Guinea to the Cone of Somalia,
From the Cape of Good Hope to the Strait of Gibraltar,
May we walk no more in paths of laughter

From the unflinching zest of Balewa and Azikiwe
To the monumental words of Nkrumah and Senghor
And the unwavering courage of Lumumba and Touré,
Blow in our hearts Mandela's peaceful ways.
Let Madiba's courage fly away with our disarrays

As the Niger's flow contrasts with Victoria's fall.
The forests of the Guinea with the Sahel's Savannas
And the heights of the FutaJallons with the Sahara's plain,
Let our shades and differences bind us like our terrain,
So Mandela's soul can forever rest in peace!

"Lampedusa, the Modern Medusa"

Lampedusa! Lampedusa!
Of snow white sands and crystal blue seas,

Europe's death bridge in Africa's Mediterranean seas,
Slayer of brave men's dreams like the Goddess Medusa

As she laments unfair neglect by her kings
So the World to those whose dreams she sinks
With unknown mirage of hope beyond her brinks.
Desperate souls' board boats of death in search of twinks,

In burst of hate like Medusa's deadly charm,
Her waves like snakes rise in angry alarm,
Her tides like the Goddess' scales lose their calm
And freeze gazes of hope into clays of sham.

Lampedusa! Art thou Medusa?
Why kill those men like the Villain, Hitler?
To save their souls from the lies that lie beyond?
A Mass grave of dreams with no street of gold to be found.

Kailey, Princess Mildred Ndelei

The Disk

In all the towns
And villages
I 've lived
I 've never found a disk as good as yours
And 'm in grieve
Of your leave.

Tonight

When you stage your war,
I tend to escape
Without my heart.
Then you genuflect
Before heaven
In silence;
With passion
And cool eyes,
With lips soft as a baby's palm,
With an eager eye
To perform ritual on my lips.
I lay in silence
For a battle of life
To receive heaven's juice.

I've Known Love

I've known love
I've known love from the earliest of times

And I've seen it flow like rivers
And flood all the rivers
In the high,
In the Sierra,
I've seen it glow
In the middle of the night

And unite like breast
On a woman's chest
Just as I'd see it creep and rattle like a snake that entangles my
feet,
Just like I'd see it pamper like the last egg on the hand.
I've seen it naked like our forefathers;
As they dandled their heads like babies on the backs of their
mothers
And I've seen it like the politics of our times:
I see it crack,
I see it dark
Like the Teye,
Like the smell of rotten meat
I watch it go wild like a lion in the jungle.

I've known Love
As ancient as Adam and Eve.

Happy Ending Is Come

Happy ending is come
I thank God Almighty,
My friends and families survived
The three plagues of humanity.

My Mother came home perturbed;
She announced an outbreak of an illness
Now in the neighboring country
Which kills in three sets of seven days.

But I was in a high spirit,
Garnished with smile
As I replied 'there is a God'
He saved us from slavery

And we've survived slavery and colonialism
And we've survived eleven years of civil war.

The wise men came from the east.
The first gun shot from the east,
The devil that danced on the Yambuku from the east

And enslaved us for 400 years,
And killed us for eleven years,
And changed our customs and traditions for two years;

There was the gunboat,
There was the AK.47,
There was the sound of siren in this new kind of war.

Then the three digits
We did not know its significant path;
Rivals shot back with 117.

For many, it was a police call:
Our girls doubled,
We became bad omen
To our colonial masters.

The sun rose again;
The throng celebrated life
And freedom.
Sierra Leone, Ebola Free!

A Cry of Hannah

From a distance,
I couldn't hear her cries;
I couldn't hear the chorus of her awful cries.

Mouth and nose filled
With the beauty she pursued
On the beachfront,
Her cry for help couldn't be heard.

Ah! A woman who mended
A woman who tended
Was raped
Was tortured

From creation,
A partner was created
For man not to be alone
But here she is left alone
By the wickedness of man.

Hannah will rest in peace
But her killers will not,
For womanhood will fight on
For a change
And create a fence
For a defense.

Rest in peace
Hannah Bokari

I Made You Cry

I made you cry
Like a baby.

Play the song please;
Reduce the volume
For a while.
Right there,
You like it
Hmm, I love it
Reverse.
Stop me like a police 'd,
Ah! Come with me
Baby, is coming.
I made you cry
Like a baby.

The song is hot!
Did it hurt?

Kainwo, JEM

Black Coats

Black coats come from the overseas
In yellow,
In pink,
In white,
And yes,
In black
To show the straightness of the jacket.
Showcase the shimmer in the black
Evidence of unfathomable IQs,
Adorned with pens
Smelling of Dior, Givenchy, Versace,
Whose very ink represents Lincoln and Annan;
Just one stroke and peace is established,
Just one dot and war can commence.
Black coats really did come from the overseas;
Charitable and full of emotions for humanity.
The all-knowing,
At least, over the coatless;
At least, over the penless
Black coats, make up the minds of the coatless.
A hand in the pocket,
Another on the table,
Brows creased
Too much heat for such small ado.
Some more coffee,
We can have sausages too,
For we are black coats
With so much work on our hands,
Too many people to help.
Our money goes back with us
And a few souvenirs will increase the luggage capacity,
But it's really back to work;
Back to the cold,

Back to more roundtables
Where only the coatless suffer.

The Tainted Petal

I
There is a song that never dies;
A song that, in the morning, shall rise
Out of the mirage of her soul
Hidden in the stereotypes of her role.

II
The song unsung stays a whisper,
Soft but loud, amid masculine litter,
A growing power in C major,
The world looks on at her labour.

III
The colour of her petal-vibrant pink,
Had dark smears of Adam's drink
Poured upon her body, soul and spirit
Tainting her body, soul and spirit.

IV
He stole her pride and it was her fault
He tore off her rights, what an assault!
Neglected and battered, she stood alone.
Can't you hear the fainted petal moan?

V
Today, golden sunrays kiss her being,
Promises of a life beyond her kin,
The notes flow from her lips for all to hear.
Sister, you will never suffer the pain I bear.

Inspiration

The morning wing
A forgotten swing
Her faint dimple
His tasteless sample
Our unsung song
Our diatribe long
Lasting and intense
The English present tense
Anything
Everything
Anywhere
Everywhere
Whatever was
Whatever is
Whatever will be
Is an inspiration.

Kamara, Fatmata Lilian

What a Smile

My smile is fake!
My smile is pain!
My smile is angry! Anguish
Filled, with grieves and rage!
My smile is frustratin'!
What a smile?

My smile is hope!
Its anxious awaiting prospect,
How then?
When you have been abused, molested
Betrayed and neglected by those scumbags.
What a smile?

I smile today, smile' tomorrow, smile forever
How?, when?, where will you?
Smile genuinely?,
Smile broadly?
With rain drops of peace?
Smile unconsciously?

E, eeeee, me? Me you ask?
When I will smile with love
Of guiltless reasons, emotions and burning desires,
Knowing that it bestows unity, peace and justice
To the bunch of misery,
Then I will smile of purpose;
Smile, smile till thy kingdom come.
What a frantic smile!

Matters of My Heart

You are the matter of my heart:
I tremble at your gaze,
My silky heart rumbles,
My tummy fumbles in doubtful rage.
I need not consult a physician,
For this physique feels no pain.

It's all matters of the heart
Yearning for conviction,
Praying daily for deliverance,
But deep and deep falls the soul.
For your youthful physique,
Each day, appeals more to my lonely gaze.

Ho! Matters of the heart.
I perspire at your touch,
I persevere to possess you,
My glee could shadow out,
Out in your absence.
So I crave daily to keep you;

You are the matter of my heart.
Without you, I desire none,
My silky heart rumbles not for another,
My tummy fumbles not for another,
My body warms not for another;
You, you alone, matter to my heart.

Beyond Her Smile

I can see her watering her garden
With tiny drops of burning rain.
At dawn, she's alert, fondling her stiff ankle to arouse
The fineness in her red eyes; sparkles.
I can see her brown teeth glittering in rage,
Her lovely paw-paw coloured skin
Now turns into dark brown.
She could have taken a pause, Swim deep in her breadth.
Yes, she could have stopped for a moment
and stretched out her rage.
But, as a wind, she succumbs to her duty,
which demands her daily;
She can't be late, no she cannot postpone,
It has to be exact and unfettered,
 Slowly, she contraflows in an unending travail.
Could she hope for a single sunny day?
Could those tiny drops of burning rains quickly dry up?
Could she ever have a day as she once melodramatised it?
Ho! Hopeful nonsense!
Better hurry to no avail
 Or else you eat the bread of sorrow.

Little Rose

Once upon a time, two lovely birds met.
Like sticker, they glued together,
In hideout, they mated .
Thousand hours, news broke;
All options where already late,
All decisions were suspended till date.
A multiple months danced by
Alas, rush hours ran by
Thousand thunders, cracked;
The sun escaped the moon
And a lovely rose came forth
 Like morning clouds, lime-tasted honey
With no lovebirds,
With no sunlight
and with little air;
Little rose shadowed out,
Then came super lovebird,
With mighty white wings
And flawless attention;
A mixture of so much tenderness,
Little rose grows, grows and glows.

Toddlers

Just so you may stand up and walk,
Yesterday you held your grip on Mama's skirt,
Yesterday you leaned on Gramma's lap;
Ho! Ya ! You pressed on Papa's toes
And you did step on those gravels filled with broken bottles and
shrapnel;
And consciously, you held on to those bricks and trees right next
to you.
But, don't worry,
No need to be scared at all.
Just don't lose grounds too early when you find your feet
or you fall and you soon know
That skirts or laps or toes you once used to stand on
will not be there for you to hold on to anymore.

Yesternight

You came in amazement,
Brought heads to your limit.
Under constant watch of depression and suppression,
We bent in prayer to our Maker.
May you go and never return;
Far, far away, from our motherland.
With what we have seen,
This is madness!
Why came to us?
You scum, you lazy fools!
You changed at the door; Chameleon to caterpillar,
Reaping where you did not sow,
Feasting on gigantic plantations,
Where farmers toiled decades, long-
Awaiting, graceful harvests.
' Think you can counteract his majesty?
You devil in sheep's clothing!
Bow now or never!

Kamara, Joseph Sherman

Speeches and Legacies

I.
Just because you've said it
Doesn't mean I believe it.
I've heard speeches and seen legacies
And can discern their differences
From the sound of the applauding crowd
Or tangible heritage that makes us proud;
By how long they each abound
Or their visibility on the ground.

II.
Your speeches are but a breath of words,
The perfect set of phrases that accords
The beauty of that heart of gold;
Your aspiration for us to behold.
They are always moving and inspiring,
Always enlightening and revealing
Well cultured and apologetic,
Richly informative and didactic.
Yet, they are just words; big or small,
Words that must be heard by one and all,
Words that reverberate across the hall,
Through the highest rooftops or domes,
Words across the streets and homes,
Across and over the hills and mountains,
All the way to the marsh and distant plains.
With flowery glamour in magnanimity
And accompanying gestures of dignity,
Each speech is another passing entity,
Smooth sound waves of capricious intensity
But always damping out with the certainty
of the morning tide, as it loses enormity,

Reluctantly shrinking down to nonentity.

I've heard speeches with promises of gold
That left me with empty dishes in the cold.
I've also seen breathtaking legacies;
The legacies of noble, tacit, visionaries,
Who, guided by bravery and humility,
Traded their souls for honour and posterity.
I've seen legacies of callous destruction
Bequeathed to ill-fated nations
By simple men who traded civilizations
For their delicate pride and emotions.

III.
So please speak, if you must
And speak not if your will is lost.
When you must speak, let the words flow
Like a spring from your heart below.
Speak up clearly on a common cause
That survives the round of applause.
Make every speech a tiny lamp post,
A common light along the coast,
To purge the shadows of bewilderment.
For 'tis in what these patches of light say
That your essence and purpose lay.
Seek to understand more than you know
And create a vision of a better tomorrow;
A vision that dries up all tears and sorrow,
With better hope to ascend from below
And surmount the barriers to grow
Beyond the fatalism we think we know.
When you discover which seeds to sow,
Trade your vision with rounds of applause
And enjoy the approving applauds.

But after you say these words,
You must remember, like Madiba,
To become the prisoner and master
Of the great vision you share.
For the profound beauties
Of the great admired cities,
Whose monuments rise high into the clouds,
Were not built by wishes made in speeches,
Nor by the glamour of their elegance.

IV.
Surround yourself with loyalty,
But do not trade the convenience
Of loyalty with the merits of excellence.
Seek excellence at every cost,
And pay for it with all your gold.
For the greatest monuments to uphold
Are the flowers, and seeds of excellence.
That you have said it
Does not mean I believed it.
I've heard speeches and seen legacies
And know their true differences.
Speeches are words; legacies are tangible.
My trust lies not in the sound of the audible
But in the texture of the tangible,
And the brilliance of the visible;
To mark the legacy of your service,
Your speeches against your legacies.

My Worst Case Scenario

I.
At the end of the spectrum, the rules have reversed.
Nothin's black and nothin's white;
all's black and all's white.
Virtues and vices run on together,
You cannot tell one from the other.
The natural order torn asunder,
The weakest defeat the fittest
and the fastest end up last;
The needy become the greedy
Then the greedy get even needier
In my worst case scenario.

II.
Of what use is schooling
When knowwho pays more than knowhow?
Society takes an ebbing dive
When diligence loses popularity.
Productivity drains in despair
When generosity becomes an obligation.
Religion loses its power of salvation
When honesty becomes old fashioned.
The trapdoor to the vortex of doom is opening up
In my worst case scenario.

III.
Neither by desire nor by choice,
Neither by punishment nor by reward,
Neither by purchase nor by gift,
But through a destiny of absolute luck,
Be it's an opportunity or a curse,
This is my heritage, my identity.
The worst case scenario!

Dreaming Shadows

I.
Dreaming shadows lost in meadows,
Transient, yet flattered like rainbows
Self aware, yet illusory
And yet so convinced of its existence.

II.
Dreaming shadows hoping for nothing.
Cast by candle, moonlight, or lightening,
They come and go; on and off,
The blessings of a flipping switch.

III.
I have a dream that's out of reach
Grappling for hope each time I flinch.
Dreaming to stay forever this time,
Yet knowing the switch will cut in soon.

IV.
In light I exist, yet exit in darkness
In each great shadow I lose my existence
Though I exist and exit for everything
Reclining in vain, craving immortality.

V.
In each reawakening cycle of the earth
Every shadow flickers away like lights on a stage.
Shadows of grains of dust or of galaxies of stars
All cling onto that single dream of immortality.

VI.
Immaterial, formless,
Unbiased and weightless,
Every shadow is but a visible illusion
and an epitome of the purity of emptiness.

A Letter to My Professor

Dear Prof.,
The past few years have been very rough;
Life, work and family have all been tough.
I've been scrambling all over for the little stuff
I need to get by and treat my chesty cough.
Yet, I've not been put completely off.

However Prof., to me it seems
This noble duty of replicating my memes
Does not lie within my frail and feeble whims.
So I surrender to daily rebukes and criticisms
With which I'm showered over sceptic gleams.
But like the monotonous refrain of epic hymns,
Or exciting fantasies of modern Western films,
This duty I'll perform in sweet dreams.

I recall your admonition
when you said that I shall,
In time, gain satisfaction
And joy above the superficial,
The absolute satisfaction
Above the social and financial
Gains, which are merely partial.

I'm sorry to say, Prof.,
That after three decades of waiting,
Lips dry from years of incessant talking,
Tired arms not so emphatic these days,
Mind disoriented towards retirement,
I do not feel so complete today.
E'en though I harbour awkward yearnings
for some partial gains I should have tried,
I'm still convinced you would not have lied.

Footprints

Footprints in the sand;
The concealed vestiges of ebbing tides
Along the absentminded beaches of the Lion Mountain,
Whose history is etched in the void of monuments
And the fleeting, yet colossal estates of the greedy.

Footprints in the air;
The fantasy of immediate convenience and the folly of flight,
Where perfect visions of hope are well-crafted and mantled up
As a mirage of expectations and promises to an evasive
tomorrow,
But today is yet another vacation to gaze the painting in the air.

Footprints of stealth;
The cold inattention through the deafening cries
From the neighbourhoods of deprivation and nurseries of
conflict;
From where, through the cries of dark sweaty faces in the
charcoal kilns
And the blistering hands of subsistence farmers, all are fed with
meals and votes.

Footprints to nowhere;
The puzzle of chaos and aimlessness, and of self destruction
From where the concrete foundations of hope are pulverized
Each day in the arrhythmia of marching steps, from generation
to generation
En route to the glamorous trepidation of the bush path to
destruction!

The Drums of Freedom

Random shots from hither and thither come
And upon the face of this lion mountain drums,
The popular rhythm of our lost freedom.
Then silent echoes of that funny symphony
Reverberate across the rain forest, lingering on
Like irksome remainders of violent storms,
The spiteful memories of appalling crimes.

These drumbeats of freedom to which we wishfully sway
Are the thunderstorms and flashes in the darkening clouds
Of the storm that takes away everything from us.
"Freedom is not free!" the freedom fighters say.
But when the price is fully paid, yet the prize goes astray,
We lose again and fall deeper into another cycle of pain.

The Dilemma of Christmas

Christmas has come and gone with all its fun,
Yet telltale signs of foregone fun still sit on the lawn,
Reminding us in turns of what good or bad we had done
In a single day.

Two days after Christmas, four days to the end of the year,
A momentous period of luxury, a yearly fear drawing near,
Festive bells fading, yet ringing with impunity feigning to care
'bout the impracticality of solutions that are New Year's
resolutions.

Predictable serenity sporadically aroused by clouds of dust
Rising in disgust, mixing with smoke from an old lorry exhaust,
Dull reminders of what festivities really cost; what we have lost
Through the recurrent minuses, from a finite wage paid in
advance.

Uncomfortably calculating the temporal distance to the next
wage
While dutifully and ruefully toying with hope on each page.
But trusting the unknown, and like a tiger in a cobweb cage,
Breaks lose, yet surrendering to the ingratitude of New Year's
Eve.

Winding Curves

Fine lines and heavy lines,
Broken lines and continuous lines:
All are but strings of bait;
Leading to your teammate,
Your bedmate,
Your checkmate
Or your stalemate.

A scanning gaze or lustful praise,
The wild geese chase through the winding maze,
In this fantasy of a fairytale:
All senses fail;
In calm or gale,
As head or tail,
This passion shall not fail.

A winding curve, up and up, spiralling above
Like a weary dove encircling its alcove:
All are but strings of bait;
Leading to your teammate,
Your bedmate,
Your checkmate,
Or your stalemate.

Gods of the Earth

I.
We are the gods of the earth,
The physical embodiment of deities in heaven.
We are the fractals of the universe;
Agglomerating particles made in the Image and Likeness of God,
Carefully composed with love and purpose one particle at a time;
Piece by piece and type by type in diversity and harmony
With mortal imperfections evened out by the choice of unity,
charity and humility,
The choice of diligence, resilience and patience.

II.
We are the beginning and the end;
Infinitely spreading the memes of our consciousness
And the accruing gains of our genes
Like dominoes of conquest in the endless stream of time and
space.
We are the drummers and the dancers of the music of beatitudes
and woes,
Unconsciously scampering through the incongruous routes of
perfection;
With the opposing voices of angels and demons in our heads,
Across the vague spectrum of goodness and evil.

III.
We are the kings, nobles and subjects
In the succeeding custody of nature and all His property.
We are the scholars and pupils of hope;
Breathlessly learning to earn the gifts of nature.
We are free to define ourselves by the audacity of our minds,
Sculpting the evolution of destinies through imagination and
choice–

The choice to be trapped in the meaningless boundaries of
heritage
Or the choice to transmit better realities and dreams.

IV.
We are the union of the seeds of desire,
The inexplicable tri-essence of the flesh, the spirit and the soul;
A finite blend of expediency that precedes and succeeds itself.
We are the enigma of mortal vanity,
A prison of sensual mortification and infirmities, the temple of
perfection
Where the soul is schooled and nourished or impoverished
Before its final liberation into eternal perfection
or death.

Kamarah, Sheikh Umarr

Homeless-ness

It is not the absence of
A roof over a head,
For
A roof there is over
A prisoner's head
But Prison is not his Home.

It is not the absence of
A back door, a front door,
For
A front door, a back door
There are
In the Magistrate's Court
But Home, the Court is not
To the Magistrate.

It is not the absence of
Food on a table,
For
Food there is on
Cookery shop tables
But Home,
The cookery shop is not
To the owner or customer.

It is not where one was born,
For
In a manger
Jesus was born
But
Manger is not Home
To Jesus.

Home is
A feeling of security,
A wholesomeness of being;

Home is
The freedom to think freely,
 Freedom to speak freely,
Freedom to walk freely,
Freedom to choose freely;

Home is
A feeling of protected-ness,
Breathing the air of Justice,
Inhaling fairness;

Home is
The roof of Vision
supported by the walls
Of accountability,
Along the warm corridors
Of Democracy.

I want to be Creative

I want to be creative:
To be creative
About the gun in fatigue hands;
About boots
On the ground of farmers.

I want to be creative
About the dark cloud
Hanging over
A community of farmers,
Where
The love between hoe
and soil,
Cutlass and shrub,
Fill the stomach.

I want to be creative
But the dust raised by
Boots on the ground
Chokes my creative impulse.

I want to be creative about my rights,
The rite of birth gave me.

How can I?
How can I be creative
With my voice
In the mouth of a gun?
How can I be creative
With my brain;
With a boot on my head?
How can I be creative
About my rights

When the gun rights the boot
And bullets smash light?

I must create
My creative-ness
In the words of my condition,
Faithful to the Theme.

To in Shay Tivi (The Krio Version of Andrew Marvell's *To His Coy Mistress*)

Ah ya, bebi, if wi bin gɛplɛntitɛmna dis Wɔlya,
Dis kɔtyangaya so, titi, nɔfɔ bin mɔna mi o.
Wi bin fɔsidɔm, tektɛmtɔkbɔtusaywi go go
Waka ɛn bit tɛm;
Yu bin go goɔldiwena Ganges rivana India
Go lukfɔjɛmdɛm; we mi bin go de na di Humber rivana England
de grɔmbul. A bin go
Lɔvyutɛniyabifo da Flɔd we kɛr Noah in bot go, bin kam;
ɛn if yulɛk, yu bin fɔ de marateJumantɔnKristɛn.
ɔni, mi lɔvfɔyufɔ bin de grokɛlɛkɛlɛtei big pas ɛmpaya.
A bin fɔtek wan ɔndrɛdiya de prez
Dɛnyubɔlyay de nɔmɔ, ɛn de kɔleyufɔrɛd;
Tuɔndrɛdiyajɛsfɔkɔleyu wan bɔbi we kaklɛkrɛpmangronatik,
Bɔt a bin go spɛntatiiya de kɔleyubɔdi;
Datnalɛk wan iyafɔ wan pat pan di bɔdi,
ɛn a bin go spɛn di las iya pan yu at.
Wetin du, lɔvin, yu fit gɛt dis lɔv,
ɛn mi go giyu di lɔv we yudizav.

Bɔtbiyɛn mi a kin de yɛri we
Da tren we nemTɛm de wisul de kam wit spid;
ɛnɔlyandabifowi, nabebrebe
Dray dray land nɔmɔ a de site go.
Wɛnyu go lidɔmna da kɔfin we mekwitmabul
Nobɔdinɔ go si da yu smut bɔdiɛnfaynfes de, ɛn
Mifaynfayn sing ɔl go gobɔnfi; bɔtwetin go mɔna pas ɔl,
Na we nawɔrɔm go gotek da tin we yu kip ɔl dis tɛm,
ɛnyugudgudɔna go tɔn to dɔst,

95

ɛn di filin we a kip na mi at fɔyu go tɔn to ashis.
Di grevnafaynehnprayvetples,
Bɔt a nɔtinkpɔsin de malanɛyanda.
Diafɔ, naw we yuyɔngɛnfayn so lɛk
Udatimbɔdiengɛl de rɔbɔyl pan ɛvri de,
ɛnlɛk we di fayainsayyu sol
De pip nayu skin so,
Na nawwifɔ rap togɛdaɛntɔn to wan;
ɛn, lɛkyuba we de fɛn tin fɔ it
Lɛwigɔmɔndayz di tɛm we wigɛt
BifoTɛmkamkamankɔfwi wit in pawa.
Lɛwitekwiɔltutrɛnkɛnswitswɛt
Rolɔltutogɛdamek wan big bɔl;
Lɛwi ala ɛnchɛrplɛzhɔ in lapa
Opin get fɔ go usayswitlayf de.
Dattɛm de, we winɔebul tap San fɔkamɛn go
Wi go mekirɔn.

Kargbo Brian Sitta

If Love

If love had eyes
It would have seen Cupid's arrow:
The anguish of dogmatic lovers,
The foolishness of craving,
The lust in mortals,
Love should have seen deceit…

If love could talk
It would have denied 'fakers':
It would tell us who cares and who doesn't,
Maybe, it would have told us who first betrayed it and
Who defiles it chastity,
Why it suffers me…
By now, it would have answered all our questions.

If love had ears
It would have quickly suffered deafness
From the issues of sinners
Who pests it with fairy tales…

If love had arms
It would embrace all mankind:
All races, ages and faces from varying places.

If love had a heart
It would have meant its love:
It would have loved,
Or maybe, it would have been biased,
Love would have understood our plights,
It would have been conscious of stress.
If love had a heart it would have saved me from the very many
deaths I've died,

It would have sacrificed its soul for me,
It would have accentuated virtual peace.

If love could understand
My pain,
My groans,
The unfortunate riot in my head,
The turbulence in my loins.

Love is bombastic but not realistic,
Promising, but not all encompassing,
Supercilious of hate
But, oblivious of fate.

School Boys

School boys now tend to be bad,
Playing pranks on girls and making them sad.
"I love you," "I miss you;" those are what they say
But they just want to get you, for an hour or day.

They may be gentle, sweet and charming
But lust for their honey lips will leave you crying.
By their looks, they're handsome, neat and cool
But don't give in! Be careful!

Although some girls are just like them,
With different kinds of lovers like books to a pen.
Their 'modus-operandi' they regard as necessary,
To have erotic partners they see as lovely.

As school going children, learn to love your books!
Don't be keen on lovers, they may be crooks!
ABC, 123, those are what you should know,
Don't follow those cunning mortals; it's your boat they'll row!

I Will Kill a Lion

Today, I will kill a lion
Whether big or small;
I will kill a lion.

I'm ready for its paws;
Sharper than knife,
Or its deadly teeth,
Capable of tearing stone,
Or its face,
That drives men to their early doom.

Many times have I scared death,
Even pain denies me.
A lion's roar mustn't shake me.

Today, I will kill a lion.

I will light a fire,
Sing sweet songs,
Face a lion, and kill it.

Haunted by this lion
In a hungry attack,
In red robes,
With death sitting on its face,
At the apex of my youth,
As a prey in its eyes.

But, I must kill this lion.
Not as Samson,
Nor as Hercules,
But as a crippling child,

Sunk in naivety,

I touch its head,
Feel the roughness of its mane,
Hold its neck and slit it.

I would kill a lion;
A lion is dead
Today, I killed a lion.

This Is Our War!

Trekking miles to motherhood,
In persistent dragging attitude,
Weariness details her unbreakable skin
But her haughtiness and difference make her faith spin

In a system plagued with mortality
She portrays sanity.
"On this bed kings are born,
On this bed queens have gone,
On this bed I must survive;"
She mumbles

Like a leaky unstaunched wench,
Fragmented thoughts of victory cloud her mind.

Disconnecting herself from the irregularities
She dreams of her child;
Her President; her future.
She must hand with health illuminates,
Rotten facilities should not intimidate.

Safe motherhood breeds better livelihood.

As if welcomed to feast,
Her foetus beams and kicks obliviously;
Totally unaware of its battles.
It makes an obdurate victory
Into evil,
Into the hands of naive Nightingale,
Into a worry world.

After greeted with affection,

Children have wept.
After yelling with passion,
Some gems have slipped
Through the paws of poor services,
To the jaws of fake promises,
The child and its mother die
The land and its men guise.

It is our war, let's fight it!

Kid's Story

Let's dance in the rain,
Let's dance out our pain.
The rain is our brother;
He makes all things fun.
Even as we wonder,
We wrestle and we run.

Old people are jealous,
They cannot be like us.

The rain has a drumbeat,
Those only children hear.
He tells us a secret,
One we take so dear.

We keep waiting for the rain,
We want to jump out again.

Rain, can you come every day?
We children want to play.

Konteh, Iyerich Bomkapr Eva

The Life I Live

The life I live,
A moral deep-decree;
The air I breathe,
Chaste and forever free;
Not a second-sum, they belong to Thee.

The struggles I've faced,
The struggles I face,
The mighty epitome of Thy grace.
That I work in the dark, it seems to me
I footle not, Yee abide in me;
The struggles overcome,
The struggles succumb,
Overwhelm me, make me strong,
Sing me a song.

Only my starry eyes see not
Thy steadfast love ceas's to rot
Thy compassion unravish'd,
Mercy endures on end
Pillow'd victory,
My footstool, my Adversary.

A life to Christ worth more my rhythm,
Much like the 'Author and finisher...' hymn,
Much love, unconditional,
Much care, undenominational,
Long-suffering,
Fore-bearing,
Much Lily
Uncountable;
Unparallel'd.

Life with Him, nev'r the same,
Nev'r again,
Nev'r a game.
But fortune, fame,
Beautifully bind like grain
All unageing glory to His name.

Mansaray, Khadi

They Came to Free us

They came to free us,
So they said:
The cattle 're dead; our men lay dead;
Our daughters raped; and our sons had fled.
Crops were gone and hunger came;
Our dreams lay in the ashes of our homes;
But yet they came to free us.

Spare a Thought for Me

Several battles of terror in war that no one had won;
They freed us from dignity,
They freed us from safety,
From the grace that me, woman and the strength that makes you
man,
They freed us from all honour.
Spare a thought for the big-headed child
Who trouble always finds
A hundred lawbreakers shall go free,
The big-headed child will be searched,
Games of chance she never wins
But draw lots and she'll be in.
All she needs is to be loved,
But remains forever lost.
Spare a thought for the big- headed child;
Spare a thought for me.

I Refuse

An unwanted stranger came to visit.
He took my hands and did not ask my permission,
Now I can't do what I used to find easy.
Something precious was taken from me:
I became dependent;
I feel less of a being;

I mourn the loss of
what that stranger took from me.
That stranger was called
Stroke!

I mourn the loss but I refuse:
I refuse to follow;
I refuse to let you name me;
I refuse to let you shape me;
I refuse to let you shame me;
I refuse to be reduced!

As long as I have a soul,
I still belong to me.
Simply I refuse!
I am Khadija,
I will not bow!

Woman

Woman I am;
Goddess divine,
Goddess greatness,
Woman....from a mighty tribe of curves,
I am life that never dies...

Present in all things living,
Woman I am.

Woman I am;
Goddess divine,
Goddess greatness,
Woman....from a mighty tribe of curves,
I am life that never dies...

Found in all things living,
Woman I am;
Creator of miracles,
The heart, the beginning, the womb, a fruitful garden, the light, a
builder, a healer,
Warrior's blood.
There is no wound I cannot heal,
From within I unearth
A mighty tree of strong roots,
I'm part of this tree;
Solid, rooted, tangled, tucked deep...
This tree I am
Ancient and new
In my curves, a song singing out strength!

A mighty tribe of curves;
A fine creation of Beauty, strength, purpose, wisdom,
magnificence and greatness.

A Symbol of love,
A symbol of power,
A signature of presence,
...Never to forget
A fruitful garden, the light, a builder, a healer...

A giver of love.

Sankoh, Osman Alimamy (Mallam O.)

Listen to Mama

When Mama said this,
I said that.
When Mama said that,
I said this.
I went out with friends,
I buoyed my head in the air,
Whistled a song,
Swung my head,
Twisted my shoulders,
Wriggled my middle,
Jumped as I walked,
My hands in the pocket.
My shirt starched, ironed to cut,
My trousers, a lawn they could mow!
My face, I saw on my polished shoes!
But...
I suddenly faced a wall,
No door, no window!
Couldn't even withdraw,
Couldn't swing my hands again,
No one to help!
I felt helpless, left alone.
I heard my mother's voice,
'THIS!'
I smiled and said THIS.
'THAT!'
I smiled and said THAT.
I saw a hole through the wall,
I put my index finger through it.
The wall slid to the side,
I leapt free and straight home!

The Anthill

I followed my mother to the farm
And there I always wanted to see;
I sat day long to watch,
I promised not to blink an eye:
Never believed their might;
Never believed their determination;
Never believed their spirit of collaboration;
Never believed one at a time could do it
All by themselves.
I wanted to be sure,
I wanted to see,
I wanted to document,
Then I fell asleep.
When I woke up,
I saw what I didn't see before I dozed off:
The hill had progressed,
My tape rule confirmed it.
My gosh! How could I miss it!
They are too tiny to be this powerful,
The ants and their hills
To me it remains a miracle
How they can build a hill my height.
Humans, adapt the ants' strategy
And build a hill of love for your people.

At Last, INDEPTH Counts Me
(so do I matter now?)

I saw it happen; many times,
My neighbours died at home,
Buried immediately!
What killed them?
Why expect me to know?
They are born, they grow up, they fall ill...
They die!
Isn't that natural?
Does anyone care about us?
We are far away from the city,
No one bothers to come to us,
We can't afford hospital services,
In fact, too far away!
Can't afford white man's drugs,
Can't afford mortuary costs,
So, we die today. Please bury us immediately!
We don't matter, so let us go.
Good health doesn't seem to be a right
For many of us.

What? Why are you here?
What do you want to do with us?
To add to our poverty and destitution?
So you wish to tell the world about us?
Tell lies to add to our misery?
He came many years ago and left;
Never back!
And you?
Like him?
Not again!
Please go away, will you not?

OK, if you insist to stay,
Here's a broken chair, if you care to sit.
There's a shade over there.
Tell me what you want.
Sorie, give them water.
Fatu, give them the rest of the maize food.
They say, we should be counted;
They say, we will matter.
How?
They say, they know the big men in town;
They say, bit by bit our voices will be heard,
Through resach, restach, re...
R-E-S-E-A-R-C-H?
Who needs to know about us?
If they say so, let's take a listen.
How great! At last we will be counted,
So tell me, will we matter?

With a bowl of paint,
They numbered our huts.
The children surrounded,
And spoke out the numbers aloud,
And clapped,
And danced.
The visitors rolled out papers.
They had pens and pencils ready.
Some had voice recorders.
And they asked us questions.

Do I remember when I was born?
Funny people!
My mother remembered the year
Everyone lost their goats to some disease,
That's the year I was born.
My three children, I know,

119

My wife, I don't know,
My uncle, I don't know,
My aunt, I don't know,
My nephews, their dad is dead,
My nieces, their parents ran away.
What I know is this:
Struggle to feed my household,
So why count me?

Come to the Community Centre at 6pm!
The village crier summoned.
The village gathered.
The Chief introduced the guests, the researchers.
Among them,
My son, Sorie, field supervisor.
My neighbour's daughter, Aminata, medical doctor.
This is new, our own are researchers!

Sorie stood up to speak,
Presenting results to us.
Let us listen, please let us listen!
He was born here, he knows here, he understands here.
Wait, malaria can be prevented?
It's not the devil who kills our children?
We should sleep in bednets that are treated?
They will give us the nets?

Things are changing, our own are part of the counting.
I am counted, we are counted.
So in the city, they know our numbers in the village.
They know how many boys, girls, babies, old people
Live in our community.
They know about our work, our schools, our social activities!
Hmmmm, but they know everything o...
No confidentiality again?

Sorie said we should not worry, they'll protect it.
We are happy!
We are no longer invisible.
They count me.
They count us.
So I matter.
We all matter now.

When a Creeping Potato Responds to a Standing Cassava

A. Cassava, grown in Warima:
I know that I'm thin but I can grow tall;
I stand and let all of you see where I am
Look at my body and see the wonderful shape I am:
My head is made up of magnificent hands of leaves,
My feet have toes that you can only marvel at.
And what I give to the world?
Pluck my leaves, and ask a Sierra Leonean
How delicious a sauce you can get out of them!
Uproot my toes and ask around
How you can eat me raw, get foofoo, gari and
A lot more out of them...
Even their cloth is good for animals to feed
And you?

B. Potato, grown in Warima:
My friend, my friend, why so conceited?
We can grow together, can't we?
Yes, I lie down but can creep from place to place,
But you? You can stand, but can you walk?
Talking about leaves?
Ask the same Sierra Leonean about me;
How delicious my leaves are!
About toes?
Haven't you heard about sweet potatoes?
My cloth performs the same as yours to animals.
In fact, humans eat my cloth as well. But yours?
I will leave it to all to tell you about what can be
Done with me.
My friend, let's remain friends
We all play our roles!

March 8: My Mother Doesn't Know

Does she know what day today is?
Does she know when it was agreed on?
Does she know who took the decision and why?
Does she know what to do today?
Does she know that some women are fighting for her rights?
Does she know that today is a day for women's voices to be
heard?
What does 'general awareness for women' mean to her?
Yes, my mother in the village has accepted it that long.
To her, it is quite normal.
Was there, is there and will there be an
alternative to male control of female?
She has never tried to answer this question.
She does not have time to think about it.
Suppression or oppression of women, what does it mean?
Her children must be fed, daily.
That's important.

In the morning.

As I was in my mother's womb in Africa,
I saw my mother hold a hoe;
I saw a bowl on her head;
I heard her talking to my brother on her back,
As she galloped us a mile barefooted to the farm.
She made a bed for him and gave him something to eat.
My brother did not see my smile as we were leaving him.
I prayed to God to protect him.
As my mother bent down to sow some seeds,
I saw an ant take away the first.
I told my mother but she was humming a song.

In the afternoon.

She gathered a few sticks to make fire.
It was very hot.
She went to the hut,
Where my brother was asleep, tired of crying.
She made food, hurriedly.
I didn't know why.
She ran with me around to gather some wood;
She picked up my brother,
Put the bunch of firewood on her head,
And galloped us quickly home.

In the evening.

It became clear to me why she was in a hurry.
My father was attending a meeting somewhere,
In a village close' by.
He should find food at home on his return.
Oh men of Africa!
Why not be a bit more reasonable,
To my mother who is carrying me all the way?
It is true that my father also did some work,
But he always had it easy to walk to the farm.
He would hold a machete and that's all,
He would stop on the way to discuss the politics
of the village with friends.
My mother had me, my brother and a bowl or something else.
In the morning,
In the afternoon,
And in the evening.

On this day,
I think about my mothers, my sisters, my aunts and all women,
Especially in Africa and elsewhere in the world;

Especially those who still have it like my mother;
Those who spend all day looking after their children;
Those who must stay in backyards when decisions are to be
taken;
Those whose office is 'destined' to be the kitchen;
Those who have just accepted things that way;
But also those who want things to change.

On this day,
As you 'enlightened' women try to make your voices heard,
I stand up to give you my support.
You may not hear or see what I do,
But you surely will!
My wife and daughters will join you in your fight,
"One day is one day"

The Dancing Africans

Not any kind of hunger, thirst, deprivation, and poverty can take it away from them. With or without slippers, sandals, canvas or other shoes, nothing will hinder them. Topless or not and with children abandoned, no sun or rain will stop them. The children copy the vibrant posture of the youth, while the aged do it slowly and they forget for a while the problems of the day. Palm-trees cry in pain as their arms are lynched from them, to provide protection against sun or rain; but also to signify in kind, Jesus' arrival in Jerusalem.

Mention here is neither about Jesus nor about Jerusalem. It is about an African leader assuming the office of the president in an African country. In addition, I am talking about the dancing Africans who are always in the streets, dancing to welcome a new African leader. Elections or no elections; democratic, undemocratic or coups, the African is ready to dance to welcome a leader with or without an obscured personality; with or without proven commitment and loyalty to their country; with or without practice with transparency, accountability and leadership. Come a new leader in Egypt in the north; come one in Ethiopia in the east; come a new leader in Sierra Leone in the west; come one in southern Africa; and come another in the Central African Republic - put on your TV and you'll see Africans dancing as never before!

How much I hope that this dancing will now be rewarded by an appropriate "thank you" in kind by the leaders for whom the Africans dance!

Who says the Africans don't have any artistic acumen? Send him to Africa to listen to the new songs that are written and sung about the new leaders. Give him bigger ears to hear the drums, the horns, the balangies, the rings, etc. that are played. Open his eyes so that he can see the complex body-work that the Africans produce as they dance in joy and with abysmal expectation of how they will live better lives under this new leader. Give him extra lenses to see the new pictures of the smiling leaders that are painted on walls, everywhere graffiti of a kind!

Yes, the Africans are strong to dance. What they have enough in them as they dance are the hopes and wishes that this new leader will bring them a positive difference this time!

I would like to revisit colonialism at its peak. Did the Africans dance for their white rulers? I don't know. Did the Africans in Apartheid South Africa dance?

Should the Africans think twice about dancing to welcome a new leader? Wouldn't cold-shoulders send volumes of messages to new African leaders that, a dance, from now onwards, can only follow when a leader has delivered the promised goods?

Sesay, Oumar Farouk

Outbreak

Her anguish anchored on the lens,
Every bit of her broken death broken to pixels and screened on
monitors,
Images scuttled between montages of a shattered Syria and
tormented Yarzidis snared at our beings;
From China to Cuba, images of a broken girl gasping for breath
crippled the air waves.

Pain latched on her eye lids,
Lurching with every wink,
Digit by digit, to touch screens,
Sending a mayday to distant shores.
Her lament lashed across the land,
Ricocheting in places flung
Numbed,
Doomed,
Shattered.
She stood at the dusk of dawn, broken.
Her eyes beamed down to pick the pieces
She lurched from bits to pieces
To piece a broken calabash.
Lenses picked her picking:
Agony exposed, spirit shattered and tossed to the wind,
Her land like a virus river, swallowed her
When she was just like Tumoe's wet clay undone.

Reign of Ruin

If we had left the birds in their abode,
tittering from foliage to shrubs with a song
and the flowers also left to blossom
so that birds would flutter, bees wheeze
and the wind blows their songs to our souls;
If we had left the rain dripping on the canopy of trees
to cascade to the shrubs underneath and
quench a thirsty land gulp by gulp
before it flows to the creeks below;
if we had left the vegetation to flourish
 on mountain tops luring the rain to the soil
like a suckling child to her mother's nipple;
If we had left the wetlands wet to sponge off excess water;
If we had left the valleys unclogged;
If we had left the waterways unblocked;
If we had left the boulders of Leicester hills untouched
to pillar the hills like the columns of the Colossium;

If we had left Samba Gutter alone to be just a gutter
and Kroo Bay just a bay and Kaningo River
 just a river flowing its course;
If we had left the Aberdeen Creek unpolluted;
If we had given back to nature an iota of the bliss it gave us;
If we had stopped the flood of flaws,
we would have watched the water flow
 to the ocean as we danced in the rain
singing the rain song we sang yesterday.
But we struck first with all the strokes of our defects,
Then on September 16th, nature struck back,
Muffling our rain song,
Miming our rain dance.
We were left to sing a solemn dirge

And danced a dance of death
In the reign of our ruin.

The Realm

The judge sold a piece of justice in his chambers for his summer holiday
Thinking there is no harm done in selling a small piece;
The police sold a bit of favour on the highway to feed his home
Thinking there is no harm done in selling a small favour;
The teacher sold some marks to students in school to pay his son's fee
Thinking there is no harm done in selling small marks;
The soldier sold a bit of discretion in the front to buy medicine for his wife
Thinking there is no harm done in selling a small discretion;
The business man bought some preferential treatments at the customs to clear his container
Thinking there is no harm done in buying small preferential treatments;
The politician sold a bit of everything in small bits and chunks to buy votes
Thinking there is no harm done in selling a bit of everything.
One day, all the vendors woke up to clearance sales
In the Mall they called the Realm of the free.

Majorie Jones

I will not let go the darkness your death left behind,
I will hold the darkness next to the light your life gave us;
I will not let go the pain of your parting,
I will hold the pain next to the pleasure your life gave us;
I will not let go the sorrow of your death,
I will hold the sorrow next to the joy your life gave us;
I will not let go the tears of your death,
I will hold the tears next to the cheers your life gave us;
I will not let go the emptiness your death left behind,
I will hold the emptiness next to the abundance your life gave us;
I will not let you go away from our lives
Because you gave more to life than death could take.

Sheriff, Mohamed

The Bug

Sex bug
Centuries old
Crawling from the pages of Nafzawi
On the loose
By the hands of scheming Crojimmy
Biting souls
Inducing high fever
Madness
Pent up passions
Surging forth
Spiralling out of control
Tsunamiclismic
Back and forth across the Atlantic
Tongues and hearts unleashed
Baring never-before
Thoughts and feelings
Locked deep beneath
Years of layers of
Pent up cravings
Tossing head through clouds
Above the skies
Floating, floating,
Gliding, gliding
Euphoric
And then...
Was there
A crash like from a coffee high
A hangover low
Or just a waking up?

The Last Mɔndɔ

Dark night
Hungry night
Harvest lean
Season mean
Multitude of souls hunger lean
There was Sasumy and Elder Bakory
A single bowl of rice lean
Spiced with red palm oil and dried fish bony mean

On Authority of Eldership
Bestowed by Communal Code
His Greyness
Elder Bakory
Slick
Mean
Shooing away Sasumy, hungry lean,
Divided and ate the eldership share
As we watched with eyes
Envenomed by eternal deprivations,
Divided our share,
Ate;
Divided again Third Time,
Ate
Till
The
Last
Mɔndɔ.

Lone fish bone needle lean,
Deathly mean
Barbed with evil-eyed venom
Charged by a million cries of souls deprived
Pierced eldership gullet clean

Slowly, agonizingly
Choking life force away.

To trump death,
His Greyness induced volcanic eruption
Swept waves up his throat
From stomach pit
Through mouth and nostrils
Gushing came
All our share,
All his share,
All what sat there before spattering ground
All around.

Stubborn fish bone needle lean,
Deathly mean
Barbed with evil-eyed venom
Charged by a million curses of deprived souls
Stayed gullet stuck.

His Greyness Elder Bakory lay still
Mouth gaping,
Tongue lolling.

We too lay still
Watching,
Deathly weak from marathon hunger
For helping or caring
With just enough strength of humour for chuckling
As Sasumy' tail-wagging returned hungry
Bitchy
Lean
Mean
Lapping up God-given supper of eldership slush
First from ground,
And then licking the eldership mouth clean

Out
In
And for spiteful assurance,
Raised one hind leg,
Squirted steaming acrid jet
Into eldership mouth and nostrils
Flushing any residual slush,
Not leaving a morsel lean.

Taqi, Fatou

The Joys

The joys of motherhood
The struggles, the pain, the stress
The ailments, attachment, dependence
Ultimate? ...
The love, the cries, the smiles
The sorrows of otherhood
When bad, t'is mother
'When good, t'is father
How fair? How fair?

Appendage

Somebody's daughter
Somebody's wife
Somebody's mother
WHO AM I? WHAT AM I?

Unspeakable- (inspired by 'what did you say 'bout colored pussies'-Hettie Gosset)

Rape no complaint
Incest no cry
Fuck no pay
Cut no feel
 Die all cry

Mother Hen

Cannot eat, have to worry...have they eaten, had enough, full?
Cannot sleep, have to worry...do they want some more, are they well?
Cannot go, have to worry...they need preference, are they neglected?
Cannot work, have to worry...do they need something, save money, where's money?
Cannot shop, have to worry...cannot afford to buy clothes, shoes, toys, books,
Worry, are they safe? Are they being bullied? Are they normal?
Worry...needs, wants

Shoulders

Broad shoulders, big shoulders
Fat shoulders, strong shoulders
My responsibilities, home expectations
Kids' want, husband's needs
Mother's hopes, father's claims
Sister's jobs, brother's asks
Broad shoulder, big shoulders
Fat shoulders, strong shoulders

Diaspora

The feat to fit
My home? NOT HERE!
I speak? No! DONT!
 I work? NO!
I look? OH! NOO!
I fit? OF COURSE NOT!
I belong? CERTAINLY NOT!
U different! U different!

Mother

Mother?
Tormentor-mother?
Judge-mother?
Nurse-mother?
Maid-mother?
Bank-mother?
Cook-mother?
Mother? Mother? Mother?

Sex

What is it?
Food, drink, weapon?
A need or a want?
Enjoyable/pleasurable? Yes!
Always? No!
Convince for sex
Ridiculed for sex
Coerced for sex
Threatened for sex
Blackmailed for sex
Forced on sex
Frowned upon for sex
Laughed at for sex
Disgusted at for sex
Frustrated for sex
Killed for sex

The Expectation to Please

Why I am expected to please?
Why should I please?
No will to please
Don't please I leave
Dress up, smile, laugh
To please
Cook, clean, bore
To please

Reclaim

Years gone by
Time gone by
Youth gone by
Strength gone by
Dreamz gone by
At loss?

Catch the years
Catch the time
Catch your age
Catch your strength
Catch your dreamz
No regrets!

Taylor, James Bernard

Ruthless Pleasure

Blood streamed down
As he armed himself again and again,
Pushing forcefully,
Unsatisfied,
Through the crimson path
with apologetic grin.

The gods begged him to forgive,
Aliens gave him confidence
To bully and tread underfoot
Mankind's weaker being.

With sightless eyes,
she begged for mercy and forgiveness
But the demons seemed to rage the more in his head:

Snarling,
Swearing,
Cursing.
He pushed again and again through the unwelcomed path,
Debris sprouting everywhere

More blood and tears bathed his face
As he pursued nature's priceless goal
For a few minutes of raged pleasure,
When all conscience is given a back seat in the faculty of the soul.

Yes,
after those few minutes,
the devil is satisfied and he collapses in his success

But alas,
in its wake

151

is eternal destruction of the body and soul of mankind's weaker
being;

Alas, when sanity returns,
He hated those few minutes
But, what has been done cannot be undone.
Mankind's weaker being trampled again.

Should it be so?
No! No! No!
Consensus is the key to such pleasure,
with smiles and deep thoughts of love
Not forced moanings and groanings
In reckless abandonment.

Pleasure should not be ruthless
But should have the attributes of Ruth;
patient and understanding
As she journeyed to the promised land
in consensus with her mother-in-law.

Ugly Rapist

You seek satisfaction and domination
your taste buds yet unrewarded
you want to taste, suck, and chew what is not yours
Shameful!

I look at you
I can't understand why you should behave like this
and give all men a bad name
Disgusting!

Brilliant succulence stares at you
As it stares at all other men
But why should you take by force what is not yours
Thief!

You take her pride away
You take her soul away
You take her dignity away
You take her life away for a few minutes of pleasure
Foolish!

You are the pride of Satan
But you will rot in the abyss of eternal flame
You merciless wretch
You ugly rapist.

Without Clothes

True friendship is when you hold dear
Someone with whom you dare to bare
In the eyes of a true friend
Your whole being can be transparent
As if you are without clothes.

True friendship demands nothing in return
Only wishing that you understand
Genuine feelings through your soul
As if you are without clothes.

True friendship is sometimes dotted with sparks
Vicious embers ready to consume parched leaves
When that happens
A reservoir of sincerity will heal feelings
As the Balm of Gilead
And you can look each other in the eye again
As if you are without clothes.

True Friendship will understand your travails
When the world misunderstands and misjudges you
With meaningless actions and absurdities
Putting on a coat of many colours.

True Friendship will understand the real you
As if you are without clothes.

Stay the Course!

Tired hands,
Powerful gladiators of the mind
Hovering over delicious masterpieces,
Tempting the taste buds.

Go for the kill…
Mmmmm, it tastes good,
Yes,
I've been longing for this the whole day:
One, two, three spoonful;
One, two, three gulps.

Then,
Dreams…dreams….dreams,
Stars playing hide and seek in the heavens,
Hiding underneath my plate,
The mirror of wandering thoughts.

Then,
The hands search for the mouth
That has gone to munch fantasy
In the weightless abyss,
Finding no support from the brain.
The jaws slacken as teeth refuse to grind their prey:
Five, ten, fifteen minutes;

The food still awaits execution,
The plate wanting to run away
To seek solace on the floor

But no!
The eyelids spy the plates slipping away;

You go nowhere,
Stay the course,
I should finish what I started;
Munch, Munch, munch away
But now too cold to enjoy,

Goodnight.

Touching the Horizon

My friend spoke to me;
Whispering in the dark,
Drawing my attention,
Speaking of the untold and unseen,

Gazing beyond the greens,
The light drew me to the horizon.
I tried to clutch the moon
But it slipped through my fingers.

I tried again and again.
This time the moon rushed into my palm,
Its light blurring my fingertips.
As I touched the horizon,

I looked at my friend
Smiling faintly,
Straining to touch my fingers,
To have a part of what I relished,
To feel the Horizon as I did

But,
The moon slipped through his fingers,
Leaving him empty handed
As I continued to touch the Horizon.

Thompson, Celia

Is thy Member Bereaved?

O member!
Art thou bereaved
To fall thy head between the mountains?
O member!
Where is thy swollen smile
In returns for your fellow's
Feverish excited greetings?
Why art thou so cold
In the middle of the furnace?
When thou knockest
My matrix, jumped
And signaled my vulva to give passage.
Why no sooner you were enclaved,
You dropped?
O! thou wicked and ignorant member
That knoweth not the needs of the vulva;
Such, which it must be delivered from.
O! thou deaf member who heareth not the groans,
Nor counteth the moans,
Thou shalth not leave my chamber
Until thou learn to count a score,
Thou shall be vulva-cuffed
Until thou liftest thy head
And fulfill my matrix demands.
For what is thy purpose
Of coming here,
If un-businesslike?
Why waste so much juice on a withered member
Still mourning?

Where I Come from

Where I come from
the sun is shining but the day is dull,
the cocks crow, cracking
the birds; chirp! Chirp! as the dogs bark! bark!
The lion laughs as the hyena digs
the fishes die in water,
the flowers sleep too soon.

Where I come from
The moon is shinning but the fireside is cold,
Genius, if born, is killed,
Saviour, if seen, is crucified,
Fathers are shacklers as mothers are hustlers;
Dreamers, dream, dream.
Thieves are swaggers as rouges are champions,
Labourers are trotters,
With only connection in heaven
and the baboons die early.

Where I come from
The rain is heavy but the ground is dry,
Childhood is roughhood as adolescence is falsehood,
Adulthood is painhood as old age is childhood,
Legacies are stillborn.
Sex; has ex, so, foetus is hanging in the balance
To live or to leave.

Where I come from
The mountains are beautiful but the climbers show despair,
Education is in retention as protection is in detention,
Wealth is health as takers are makers,
Politics is sticky as crime is perfect,
Resources are sourced,

Justice is rusty as money is talky,
Fair is foul and foul is fair.

Where I come from
My compatriots are asking questions,
The children; who, after the placenta tears, hear their mothers'
travail;
The youth; who, searching for their worth
Know that, the noose is loose;
The adults; who, horrified at their cracked hands, stare at the
trampled eggs;
The old; who, imprisoned by despair, cry for the cloud to
swallow them.

Where do you come from?

Remember her; Hannah

What do I do with you now
in your battered, bloody body?
If your eyes were not glued,
I could watch the last pictures you saw
and tell your story differently.
What a picture you were made; when captured,
must be nominated for all the details it presents.
What did you see before they were shut?

What do I say to you now
In your drenched, drugged deafness?
If your lips were not glued,
I could have seen your last emotions
and write your story differently.
What a sight you were made; when looked upon,
must be nominated for all the aspects it presents.
What were you saying before you were glued?

Let me hug what was left of you,
For that is all I can offer you-
Justice, I do not have to offer
A $1000 might never be paid, for you, or any.
So, let me hug you, for that's all I can offer.

No one saw you when dragged, gagged, rapped and sealed.
So, I will hug what was left of you,
Cry with your mother,
Lay a flower by your troubled blood,
Light a candle for you; and then,
Wait.

My Nights & My Mornings

Come, I'll tell you about my nights.
One night can unfold in different colours; but the
grumbling clouds forewarn this night will be the 'standing one';
the stars are not here.
there will be no mosquitoes but the wolves will come sniffing for
meat;
they tear without mercy; their right, I guess.
 Hunger!
Lightening accompanying thunders and the motorists wash me
Their right, I guess.
Safety!
The waters caress my shaky legs but I am not alone
If the waters do not get my neck and I outswim the reptiles,
you will not find me on the slab.
Oh! the siren chimes.
That is another night.
But if the morning sun greets me, I will tell you about a different
night.
How is your night?

My mornings!
Hurry, my mornings are not for snails.
The slab I escaped, so, I take to the street; fist for fist
The wolves sniff from their corners; their rights, I guess.
Breakfast!
But where is mine?
Ouf! I'll have the half rotten oranges after sweeping the stalls,
some bad creditors I have here; their rights, I guess.
Profits!
The 'others' pay but they cannot put up with my smell
and they think I hail from the Ali Baba clan.
Can I say otherwise?
They can't hear me from the distance; and

if I insist, I will caress the bars.
Will you come for me?

I came to Pray

I came to pray on this pedestal
for the pedestrians
on the left, right and the others going across
their destinations I know not
but if it be beyond the seas,
I came to pray
that they will not shake off the soil from their feet
and their hearts will remain home.

I came to pray on this pedestal
to the Celestial,
for the drivers turning left, right and the others going across
that, at their stations, they will work diligently
and their hearts will remain home.

On this pedestal I came to pray
for the preys,
for swift flight from their predators
and their safe return, home.

I came to pray on this pedestal
for my pallies,
that when next we meet,
they will remember to pronounce my name correctly
and we will lick palm oil with our fingers from my mother's
kitchen.

The Dog and its Bone

The dog and its bone,
who can separate the two?
even the life of the giver is endangered
with watery eyes, it salivates and wags,
and then jumps to snatch;
it plays the giver's game until
it gets the bone between its teeth.
now, a master of the bone, it forgets the giver, and
as a hyena, it breaks and tears
like a vampire, it sucks and sucks

And then,

once the master is satisfied
and the bone is juiceless,
it gives a large belch of satisfaction
and breaks wind,
it separates itself from its spoil
and as it strolls around lazily, looking for another,
it scorns it from a distance,
leaving it to dry in the sun

And then,

On a hot, hungry, day,
it remembers; and then
master dog, with its tail between its legs,
returns to its vomit.

Thompson, Pelham Jonathan Adeleke

Flying Leaves

Another day is here.
The morning keeps coming out, extending
Its windy hands and due of smiles.
The forge of the mind is hot, and yet the
epidermis is
feeling cold.
Cold out of the warmth of memories.
Neither can we return the time,
Nor the lost moments can be found.
Tell me!
Show me
The wind that blew away the dust on wish we
built our hearts.
Pour me the rains that caused erosion on our
desires.
No, I say no!
Not even the storm can drown me to despair.
In your stream of love I will float.
Never will I sink.
Even the bitter honey you spat in my mouth
Cannot cause me to sink in mortification,
No! Not now I am bearing unbearable
burdens
And my heart is beating a rhythm to which
I cannot dance.
Only the lyrics of the music I can sing
With the voice of my tears rolling down;
Dropping on the sands of our time.
You have still not gone
Though you have left,
You have only given your back to the light my
heart produced
For you and on you

And face the dark side of your world.
That light you gave your back to,
Has gone ahead of you;
To your future.

Thulla, Philip Foday Yamba

The Coming of the Lord

For you we wait'd, O'lord
Just as ye sayeth.

In massive waves the turbulence of thy promise ripppl'd across
our shores; waves so enormous we quiver'd in uneasy
foreboding,
For who were we in the eyes of our lord that he, in his great
wisdom, should entreat for himself a moment of solitude to work
in our midst?
In the thicket of the interior; the obscurity, back of beyond, siteth
in peace, a brazen'd phoenix, rous'd from its slumber, knowing
not worth its myths 're to thee.

For you we maketh, my lord, according to thy every word,
courteously, as ye pronounc'd every instruction in ceaseless
succession,
For the harbinger sayeth:
thresh all! Ye owners, thresh your bars and thresh your pans;
tend your muffs,
make them fluff;
Tend them short! Our lord to come!

And so our fluff'd feathers we pluck'd,
The glossy ones we polish'd,
Our backs painlessly heav'd in humble service, whiles faces
sparkl'd the prospects of our lord's coming.
We plough'd; we harrow'd our land and sow'd corn in the
marshes;
Our lines we paint'd white as we did the trees, the twigs
And all else that seemeth out of sight.
Our nests we paint'd in elegant hues, as we did our backs,
For the harbinger sayeth:
thresh all! Ye owners, thresh your bars and thresh your pans;

tend your muffs,
make them fluff;
Tend them short! Our lord to come.

We took a break and took another break.
We toil'd in uneasy foreboding and eager patience, we wait'd
In joyful anticipation and glorious expectations, we wait'd,
We wait'd and wait'd, for we knew our lord was coming!

Nightingale practis'd their brilliant train of feathers and wait'd;
The chickens, the vultures and eagles did what they do and
wait'd;
We made the air so cool that our lord shall toil and not sweat;
We made the lines so level that he may ride without tremors;
We tetter'd a flock so our lord may feast after his toil;
We got the woods in a fireplace so our lord may play after his
toil.
All this we did with the last gold in our chests!

The nest, glimmer'd in hope, its shadows cast to infinity;
The muffs nostl'd to one another, tending their heads;
The herd, happy though they stay'd;
The lines pant'd tiringly in astute postures;
The bars glisten'd in solemn reflection over waning hopes;
Abodes haunt'd by solitude and somber contemplation of futility
As logs sat in blank gaze in the vacant pavilion awaiting utility
And the air sat weary but still, in silence of bewilderment.

For you we wait'd, O'lord.

The Palm tree

Look! they come scampering:
Running over hills; through forest, sunburn'd;
Through swamps and savanna plains,
From hamlets to squalids, bare-feet
On stumps they hurry,
Hopping through thick twigs,
With cynic grins,
They come;
They trot, so quick,
In haggard greens,
They come;
They plod and plod
With indefensible attitudes
And speak with such platitudes.
Listen! to their prodding;
Their discourse, crude,
Their hearts, mean,
Their cheeks glow with hungry delight.
They wander down busy paths…
To prune what I use too.

Amidst thorns, brok'n branches and ant-hills;
Up brazen'd trees, they climb,
Sometimes rack'd by tree-snakes
And hack'd down;
Landscapes pieced away,
Limpin' in the sun
To urban folks on rural hilt's delight.
Farmyards scar'd,
 Grey leaves brush'd,
Racing dogs to fair share have:
They take my fronds,
My blood they guzzle,

And blur their reasoning
But quell with broths,
My nuts, they crack and sop my fat...
And scrape beetles too.

To mend brok'n fences;
Roofs of sticks,
A power purg'd, a worm they made me fling,
A rub, a wash, a bed-mat, they made me do,
Much stimulant exert:
My stalks, my husks, my leaflets and rachis,
They spare not, but burn.
My back heav'd in strife,
Bent on projects nurs'd in unforgivable joys...
Oh! scavengers, that I use too.

To me they sing vicious 'politickin',
Declaim my fame at heydays,
Ascrib'd to spiritual and ritual ceremonies
And lay bare my phallic and ambiguous human fecundity
With all my timely, varied, calories...
But eat beetles?
That I know too.

Ode to a Fallen Hero

Many have I seen great men whose steels wrench'd in wall;
And many have I seen nations fall.
From Achilles to Homer, read in poems,
Their steels glimmer'd, men's wroth bitter songs and moans;
Ozymandias! thinks
All Great but conceit'd, their glories fall.
Even the Danes, castles-power drunk,
What's to Caesar; to Caesar's dues.

Nev'r have I seen a man of glory full;
Great leader, he made his battle a field serene to rule;
In the midst of Squirrels, his granary full;
A molten of gold; his words a spell.
A famine land, he turn'd a mall,
A greenhouse, soon he call'd a wind,
His rancour, nev'r, alas! a blushful cream;
His enemies rob and get redeem',
Though frightful choice, academe
Blithering point'd; academic
To him, so young, was much ceramic.
To academe, he'd come to be
Hail'd, a nature he'd made the scribes
Laugh'g stock.
For what's a scribe, glim and sincerity mock'?

Oh you! Odysseus mould
Of God, they cast you much a gold.
Thy words, thy bound; thy actions, nev'r rebound;
Thy gait, inward, it took a look;
Thy heart, so fix'd and rest'd; it nev'r shook.

To you com'-leaders and followers too!
Your gold; your heart and loyalty show

Your masses ev'r be;
And loyalty give, shou'd majority see.
Facade you dent,
Integrity you rent,
If forty-nine you turn
Your backs fifty-one,
Know! wisdom not in skin earn'd;
Wisdom, sincerity and love in God, you ought to bind.

Glady Lad Speaks to Little Beetle

Oh! Little Beetle,
Why allow yourself to be littl'd by tiny ants?
With such mammoth body and sharp clippers, could've us'd your mettle
To crush them all, you couldn't?

Oh! my Glady Lad,
My body, drowsy though I creas'd; my brain rattl'd,
'Unity is strength', we've heard,
It's hard
To beat a unified army.

Oh! Little Beetle,
Hard indeed to believe you're caught by such slow creatures!
With so many legs, you could've run and somewhere settl'd.
Now you lie impotent like Gulliver's ventures.

Oh! my Glady Lad,
Much as a wall-ivy,
In vain I climb'd, my nightmare ceas'd to bury,
Prodding legs and shrieking wings, my torso carried.
The finish'd line, sometimes, not on swiftness reach'd, it's seldom blar'd;
Survival fought with a body disabl'd: endurance's such a priceless synergy!
A point much shrewd in the hare and turtle of Aesop' fable.

You're not the dumb sheep,
'cause you've wav'd a leg in defiance,
You've tried not a fight; you seem asleep?
You're dragg'd into tiny hole; use your defense!

Oh! my Glady Lad,

How I wish'd I'd leap'd
My rippl'd body, so prevent a trance;
My wings, clipp'd, my legs, ripp'd,
I'm huddl'd and gripp'd.
Your voice a knell to my ears
And fills my eyes with tears.

Some Meeting Places

By the river that sits at the end of the plain,
Their secret grove roundly unfurl'd.
Marked by dead leaves, caused by entwin'd hands and
friskin' games,
That place once a thick shrub cover'd,
That shrub has long since been transform'd;
So also 're the trees us'd as shields,
Every piece a sign in their minds inform'd;
A seat they set, bright leaves and flowers for
ensigns.
That tree-on that very spot,
Her swain wait'd; their arrang'd tryst.
They spoon'd all evenings with all the energy they had,
Free from bedlam, the world offers, at least.
A day not they miss'd; prompt to meet the evening hues,
The frowsy frog and slithering snakes
Bask'd in reeks to listen their news,
The woods hush'd; trees halt'd
To take just a look.
Eros, too, had her libido shook
As a pure love came pouring forth.
Now that he's gone, that fateful night;
She shrinks, herself, she embraces,
Memories brought to life by the sight;
Memories, so great, in the mist of some meeting
places.

The Frame in My Gaze

It's a longtime now, yet it lingers,
The frame of dad; a dad long kill'd
Appears in my gaze, with head till'd.
A martinet, yet kind and loving,
There in Potoru, shot and shattered, his
family longing
For his care, for his support.
All good things perish'd
The land, wound'd, humans, weary,
A cruel, bad, country.
Men had gone to war
Mine's blood flow'd afar
In silent whispers, there comes the sound:
War's but terrible, not one a win
For good or bad, all but a sin.
None can attest, neither books report,
In a distant village, the manner of death,
Gruesome so, the war's done,
And these twenty-three years, the scenes charge,
Time rolls, seasons come and seasons ago,
Quislings change, enemies reconcile,
Peacekeepers rap up -duty accomplished.
Dad's gone, things are static.

The Brutes

Fiercely thrashing through,
Slashing what they met, my town
A ghost after which.

Wilson, Randoulph L.A.

The Voice that is Calling

I keep hearing this voice
Coming from passion's eternal abode,
Timeless musings; setting me aglow.
My heart is being procur'd.
In you I feel secur'd,
My horizon is alight'd,
Purging away the crimson'd tide.
My soul is deck'd
With the whispering
Tune of your symphonic
Voice; dispelling the solitude
Of my yesterdays; groping
Fingers easing these aches
Of long lingering void.
Your breath is a cure,
Making me pure.

An Elegy for a Continent

I hear the cries
And I grimace at the echoes
From the mountains,
the skull infested valleys,
I smell the odour
Of blood;
Of freshly slaughtered youth,
Of bodies decomposed;
Flesh, bones, blood and sweat
Of my kindred

I keep hearing the wailings,
Crescendos of grief
From heaps of graves;
From the remains
Of churches and of mosques
Terrorizing in, the air looming and
The earth, desecrated with innocent blood.
Everywhere, around me,
The voices of tortured youth and suckling mothers;
 Sliced and slain

In the sea,
Thousands swallowed
Sad gait,
The shabby clouded sun;
The silent witness
To this gale

From the Maghreb to the Great Lakes;
From the Horn to the Peninsular of Freetown;
Fields of fire in Juba, Darfur and Delta;
The contaminating air at Nyanza Ridge;

Pieces of bones plagued the Shores of Lake Kivu,
Tripoli and Benghazi hacking each other
As trails of blood streak the River Mano,
Ivory Coast turning apart as hopes dwindle
The chorus of a race in mourning;
Mount Kilimanjaro re-echoing it.
The creaking and the groaning;
The howling of my people
In excruciating pain;
The elegy of a continent
Written on the Kalahari,
Recited at the Sahara…
Grieving in my heart.

Twilight Cravings

Awaken' by your whispering cravings
Under twilight's silent raging passion;
Vainly, I resisted,
Yet, you insisted
I feel the pulse of your soul,
My heart danced to the rhythm
Of those feral fingers, then I
Petted with your filaments of pleasures
Right at the bastion of your treasures
I feel the gale of joy;
In ecstasy, soared my beloved toy.
Under your restless breath
I can tell the length
And breadth,
And depth
Of your desires.
Two colours of fires
Lie in your eyes.
You gave me the cue,
Dutifully, I followed through
Alas…
I fell under your spell,
Besotted in your hypnotic smell,
I had no option,
So I got drowned in sweet sensation.

He Prevailed

(For the Late Mohamed Bobson Kamara)

He never did succumb,
He prevailed;
He fought and conquered
On the stage
A lasting thrill, he left
Audiences in exhilarating applause
At the City Hall
And auditoria elsewhere.
His theatrical agility was reminisced;
A clement demeanour deeply missed.

He never did succumb,
He prevailed;
A first-rated speaker and singer;
Commentator, teacher and performer.
The lecture halls of Milton Margai
Still beholds his absorbing presence;
Screens, still will be adorned
With your hilarious charm,
Even as you lay tranquil and calm

He never did succumb,
He prevailed;
Counting in droves
The souls he lifted,
The hearts he gladdened,
The minds he enlightened,
In the arts, the media, the academe,
In local governance; he prevailed;
A self-effacing essence of himself he availed.

187

Yawmah, Jusu Jaka

Realm of the Free

In 1462, the waves carried the shrill cry, "Sierra Loya"!
Lion Mountains! Professed the sailor, Pedro Da Cintra
To this wonderful abode of nature, valour and power
Reduced to a mall for humans during the colonial era,
Land of the homeless, the Athens of Old West Africa.

Sierra Leone, your love in our hearts, we feel
High we exalt thee, Realm of the free.

Our scars from the Hut tax and Amistad will surely heal
On the abyss of pains and penury, we place a solemn seal
Freedom! We say to our children, as we manly show the weal
In the midnight stories; the moonlight making a perfect ideal
And in due honour, we shout your name with a profound zeal.

Sierra Leone, our loyalty to you is, and shall always be
High we exalt thee, Realm of the free.

Let the heavens shower forth blessings, let peace be still
Let the Earth open up, bringing abundant yields where we till
Let the children show love, let them all swiftly obey her will
Let freedom reign, where our forefathers paid this costly bill,

With their blood! How they paid… to us is such a bitter pill.

Sierra Leone; Unity, Freedom and Justice, our decree
High we exalt thee, Realm of the free.

The landscape is blissful, the landmarks are clearly seen
The minerals are bountiful, and their numbers are umpteen
Countless springs and fountains, the pastures are so green
In this realm, once cradled by Her Royal Majesty, the Queen;
Whose interest to this weaned child, was and is, still so keen.

Sierra Leone, your beauty is beyond what eyes can see
High we exalt thee, Realm of the free.

The sand is crystal, sparkling in all your lovely beaches
The mangoes, the guavas, the pineapples, the peaches
The luxuriant tropical rain forests expressing your vegetative riches
The fishes, the animals, the colourful birds chirping in various niches
Makes this small paradise on Earth the best among so many choices.

Land that we love, Our Sierra Leone; we shout with a glee
Great is our love, we highly exalt the Realm of the Free.

Changing the World

I woke up this morning from my sleep
Thanking the Shepherd for the dearly keep
And the tenacious care to His numerous flocks of sheep.
Faintly, I can hear the signatures; the cocks crow, the infants weep
To tell all asunder, "It is dawn!" Above the skies, I can see the sun creep
Slowly but surely, in due timing, like the proverbial turtle climbing a steep.
But I did wake up with a word,
And that is to change the world.

The sellers echoed, the birds chirped in the distance
Amidst the noisy confusion, I ought to keep my balance
And to uphold my purpose, I must buckle up endurance
With a steady focus and pace, leaving nothing to chance
My task is time-bound, every second with its significance
And the zest to conquer spews forth like a blazing furnace.

Because I woke up with a word,
Which is to change the world.

The routine is quite unusual and demanding in every way
The things I do clearly differ from those I did the previous day.
But peace was certain, and emanating from the depths of the mind.
In my dream, this peace was duly enjoyed by all; too hard to find;
Dignity, tolerance, compassion, justice and equity all combined
To give a lasting and amiable satisfaction to every human-kind.

And so strong was this word,
"We need to change the world"

The Sun is passing, dwindling my chances; twilight is in full
pursuit
The obstacles are inherent but I must keep my eyes on the
summit
My time, energy, strength, leisure, I painstakingly submit
To this lasting universal change, I kind heartedly commit
Though I strive, though I crave, though I willingly forfeit,
I must keep my gaze fixed and never yield to defeat.

So I must hold fast to my word,
To bring this change to the world.

The day is passing; I lose courage, twilight almost done!
I slump'd in total despair, thinking all hopes are gone...
And suddenly, from within, deep within me... I can see!
Yes! I've got it! My despair formed part of the raging sea,
My focus, my vision, my resolve, my energy, they all possibly
Gave beauty to my dream, and made it just what it seem'd to be.

Yes! I can! I can change the world!

Meet my dreams and uphold my word.
"The change the world needs is inside
And together we can, if we all decide
As such, you and I form the word, 'we'
But first I know it starts inside of me."

The Journey of Life

The journey of life begins with the birth of a child.
To the expectant, this is considered to be a streak of luck
When, with both hands and feet, it gives a painful knock
Like the distant blaring sound of a ship coming into a dock;

This newly born is ushered, to be counted among the flock.
Congratulations to the kindred, a warm welcome to the big fellow
I am called names; bouncing, chubby, my pie, heroine or my hero
I am loved, pampered; my presence keeps the affection aglow
To my hosts, a one in a million, and with me they feel mellow
I suck, cry, and do nothing at all, through the stages of all-Zero.

Days turn weeks, weeks become months, I feel like doing more
I enjoy being carried around, but at times, I really do prefer a tour
With boldness, I get down, trying to move with both hind and fore
Ignoring the falls, the head bumps; often times, I even sustain a sore
Though I cry, my hosts are happy to see me get down on all-Four.

The next step is so assuring like the cool of the morning dew
But I am cautioned to think and reason well in everything I do
My chances of error are great, but my demands are now few
Caught up as I reflect at my Zero days; everything seems new,
Everyone is up for a change, when I get to the stage of all-Two.

When I sometimes put on a frown, requesting for a piece of bread
I am strongly rebuked, bashed or offered a snarling scold instead

"Children don't beg!" On unlucky times, with a spank on the head,
Were the dreaded remarks, just to prepare me for what lies ahead
My early all-Two, my First decade, when the world is such a spread.

I get along, evenly, get used to the boring economics of child composure
The Oedipal madness, mixed with the labyrinth of youthful peer pressure
Good manners, etiquette, acquiring an education, ignoring my leisure
The choices, the mistakes, the motivation, the distraction, the pleasure
Make up my early all-Two, in my Second decade, in a different measure.

Laying await on my paths are chances; some plain, some, a barricade
Aiding me to take them are the choices and priorities that I have laid
Stalling my moves, most often, are the hasty decisions I must have made
Also the inherent cool I enjoy while basking under life's beautiful shade
This starts my mid all-Two, I am now in the mid of my Second decade.

Going through the thick and thin, duly propelling me to my destination
With all my experiences, I cultivate the art of making a good decision
Though at times, sinister and uncanny feelings create the apprehension
Of growing, the consequences, taking responsibility for every bit

of action
Vivid changes during my Third decade, Darwin called this theory,
'Evolution'

The paths are many; some rough, some straight, some a diversion.
So I seek a good life, a family; as such I make a solemn dedication
To a mate and confidant with whom I share a very mutual attraction
And with this, doing something lucrative with my acquired education
Still on all-Two, my Third to Fourth decade, a stage of being a motivation.

I was born to a generation; I now partake in this noble multiplication
Owing to the biblical fact and my deep sense of a family orientation,
I now stick to a life of earning and also sharing every bit of option
Approaching my late all-Two, I'm also the father of a whole generation,
Now at fifty; "I have reached my golden jubilee". I shout in jubilation.

My next move is to a point where I become a source of inspiration
I have gained, have also lost... in a world full of so much competition.
Sharing my quite moments are smiles as I look back in retrospection;
How I chose my path; partly using a guide, partly using my discretion
In my Sixth, heading for my Seventh decade. I nod in self-appreciation.

Changes are clearly evident! Now frail, slurred speech, I can hardly see,
At times with Alzheimer's disease, I even addressed my soul mate as "he".
I need a very kind hand to hold and help me get wherever I want to be,
A perfect friend, that's always by me, even when I'm taking a walking spree.
At Eighty and beyond, for a guide, I choose a stick. I am now on all-Three.

I become so dependent, to all my kindred, I'm now a very huge burden,
The time slowly passes; I am exhausted, senile, weak and heavy laden.

I think of all my past; my practices, deeds, whether a believer or a heathen,
Which will be solely suggested, not by me, but by those I called my brethren
When I finally give up the ghost… I'm grieved, sadly missed all of a sudden.

Filling my world are a huge gap, grief, condolence and moment of sorrow,
Death ends my circadian rhythm…! I now head for the valley of its shadow
For the crossover…on their arms they take me to a lonely place, six feet below
My days of all-Zero, to all-Four, all-Two, all-Three, and back to all-Zero!
From all-Zero to all-Zero… The Journey of Life ends with the death of a child.

Ode to the West Scar

The scars, penury and blithering rumours
Radiate through the whimpering wails...
Of babies, plunged in strapped bracers,
Their fading parents, gasping for an end
To the woes of fatal discomfiture
Counting the odds, of lifeless heartbeats
Shadowing on the bleak horizon
On plains, turned graves, on wet caches, where our forefathers
wept...
Go, never to come back;
Go and party with the mist of darkness
Where they laid in vomitus, and scrupulous deals
Glanced by smelly relief, amidst the dying grief

I could go on
To tell of this plague
Fading out of age
With cutting edge thinness
Of the young and sage
The helpless and motionless
The unsung heroes
The dedicated givers,
Who toiled in blood
With an unflinching peak
To salvage their quivering
Victims; of circumstances
Beyond their earthly reach.
Alas! It's a nation pitch
If they couldn't touch,
They could save as much
And if they did, bye to their watch...

Fitted is a masked protection
From a scar that beats every probing detection.
Prisoned stewards!
Clinging to fading rewards
Not for theirs, neither loved ones
Nor for heirs; then it became worse!
Body bags
Unholy ceremonies,
Broken memories...
No rights, to validate rites
Pallbearers, turned grave diggers,
Call centres, centered callers,
Plastic barriers webbed nuptial borders
Social centres turned desecrated corners
117 toppled 247.
No time to debate hell or heaven
And the rhythm of mourners
Echoed in ghostly corners...

Pity over mystery
Raids over aids
Sweats and blood mixed
On the cradle where they risked.
Theories swamped the media
When the sun dawned on donning
The narrow escape!
For each giver that tops the doffing...
Synonymous to death
The PPEs! The ETCs!

Hands, sanitized
Souls, sterilised
Emotions, hypnotised
Duties, mesmerised
Bush meat, minimised
Suspects, criminalised

Survivors, victimized
Dead bodies, demoralized
Donors, epitomized
Citizens, none socialized
As body counts maximized...

Lessons learnt, notes taken
For this scar shan't be mistaken
For the other that will leave us broken
To tethers; words, anger...unspoken
A nation that withstood; this too, shall pass, unshaken!

And then,
Did some realized...
That the scar which rose from the east
Soared through the four cardinals?
Plunging like a grisly beast
Executing by its selective tribunals...
The dehydrated victims dying with clutched fists
Left indelible twinkles in our midst
Shall dissipate like a foggy mist
On the horizon where our fathers stood
And where all shall resist with a collective brood.

Climbing the Sky

"In everything you do, your aim should always be the sky"
Was what she said to me after saying, "My son, draw nigh"
"I don't have wings, Mum", came the timid and solemn reply
Coyly, I added, "So how do I get to the sky when I can't fly?"
With a smile, said, "Even those with wings can't go that high".

Sitting all by myself, puzzled by this maxim, I noticed a little wren
The thought flashed with a plan, so I found a small book and a pen
To this plan I clung, like the precious brood of chicks to Mother hen;
A parachute or a ladder? A rope, catapult… plus some very strong men?
But one thing! How could I possibly do all of this, when I am only ten!

For my trip to the sky; I need a springboard, or maybe a strong catapult.
What if I fall? What if I…? My fears, anxiety and perplexity made it difficult,
Thus bringing limitations; to my conscience, this was the greatest assault.
So I waived this idea, for another time, maybe… when I'm a full grown adult
That's done! I amused myself with a kid rhyme, a frog leap and a somersault.

"I'll someday climb the sky". I keep saying this, with a very strong conviction
And as I transcend from a boy to youth, hold on to my childhood proposition,

Now aware of what it takes, it becomes my mantra and personal motivation
Climbing the sky, my cliché, and all the difficulties attached, my inspiration
And on that sky I'll be, while they shower me with words of congratulation.

Congratulations to make up for the effort and pains while I plan in solitude,
Also disproving my feeble apprehension by reaching the top of the latitude.
It will be amiss, failing to express my heartfelt and undiluted gratitude
To all; the failures, the fumbles, the limitations, the feeling of lassitude,
Nature, the wren, my small book and will, for proving out my aptitude,

The ten years old, the well-wisher and critic for giving me the attitude.
I reached my limits, I did it! I've made it! My climb to the sky is absolute
And there I'll declare, "The aptitude plus the attitude brought me to this altitude!"

Contributors

1. **Conteh, Samuella Julia** loved reading from a very young age, and she grew up to be fascinated with books by Enid Blyton, Mills & Boon and by mid-secondary school; she could hold serious conversations on works by James Hadley Chase and others of the same genre. As she would explain, she gets transported to distant places and believes she was actually in the plots of the books she read. With good writing skills and an easy understanding of the English Language, she ventured into writing essays, poems, prose and contemporary articles, many of which got published in local newspapers. She won a scholarship to do a distance course in Specialist Writing with the Writers Bureau, London. Samuella studied Human Resource Management and has for the past thirty years worked in several units of Office Management. She is currently with the National Human Rights Commission. She lives in Freetown, Sierra Leone with her daughter and granddaughter.

2. **Fofanah, Kemurl Mustapha Abdul** is a poet and a writer currently studying for a Bachelor of Arts in Peace and conflict studies at the University of Sierra Leone, Fourah Bay College.

3. **French, Miatta** is currently one of the five members of the National Electoral Commission (NEC) of Sierra Leone. She has previously served the commission as head of its outreach and external relations unit and as director of operations. She has always been very interested in the performing arts and entertainment generally and has appeared in various live theatre and recorded performances. Her major passion has always been for words and she believes that words must be measured like the ingredients of a dish so that meanings come out as they are really meant to be said. 'It is important to say what you mean, because meaning what you say can be compromised by your actions,' she believes.

4. **Hallowell, Gbanabom** is a poet, novelist and journalist, and founder of the Salone Writers Forum, a Whatsapp group of Sierra Leonean writers. He has published six volumes of poems, a novel and a diary of the Sierra Leone Civil war. He recently completed a seventh volume of poems titled, *The Art of the Lonely Wanderer.* Hallowell is the editor of *Leoneanthology: Contemporary Short Stories and Poems from Sierra Leone* and of *In the Belly of the Lion: An Anthology of*

New Sierra Leonean Short Stories. He holds a PhD in Interdisciplinary Studies in the Social Sciences from Union Institute & University, USA, an MFA in Creative Writing and Literature from Vermont College, USA, an Executive Education from Harvard University, and a HTC from Milton Margai Teachers College. He has taught college and university education in Sierra Leone and in the United States, and is currently Director-General, Sierra Leone Broadcasting Corporation.

5. **Ibrahim, Zakiyyah Thara** is a women's/child's-right activist, writer, artist and entertainer. She is a Sierra Leonean/American attending Rutgers University. She is a youth organizer for the fistula focused; Women's Health Organization International (WHOI) based in Canada, and has worked as a volunteer/counsellor/teacher at *the Don Bosco Fambul* Organization for abused children and supported the work of the Aberdeen Women's Health Centre in Sierra Leone. She is currently working on her first novel.

6. **Jones. Harriet Yeanoh** is a lecturer at the Institute of Languages and Cultural Studies (INSLACS) Njala University, Sierra Leone. She holds a Bachelor of Arts degree (French and Linguistics) from Fourah Bay College, University of Sierra Leone and a Master of Arts in Descriptive and Applied Linguistics from Njala University.

7. **Kaifala, Francis Ben Esq.**, LLM (Lond.), LLB (Hons.) (USL), B.L is the Senior Managing Partner in the Law Firm **Kaifala, Kanneh & Co.,** at Top Floor, 81 Pademba Road, Freetown. He is a Bilingual Lawyer and poet who writes and speaks French in addition to the English Language and a former Spokesman/PRO of the Sierra Leone Bar Association. He is a prolific writer and researcher and his legal, Finance and Economics articles and social Commentaries calling for reform have appeared in respected National and International journals, magazines, tabloids and websites. **Francis Ben Kaifala** is an alumnus of the Sierra Leone Grammar School, the Fourah Bay College and the Sierra Leone Law School. He was called to the Sierra Leone Bar in 2007 after having successfully passed the Bar Final Examinations as the "Star Pupil" and received several academic awards. He is also an alumnus of Queen Mary, University of London where he pursued the joint LLM (Master of Laws) in Law and Economics. He is currently in

active private legal practice and the holder of the Young Lawyer of the Year Award 2015.

8. **Kailey, Princess Mildred Ndelei** was born in the Southern Region of Sierra Leone in Serabu village, Bumpeh Ngao Chiefdom. She went to Saint Andrew's Secondary School Bo and presently pursuing higher education. She is a young poetess whose online publications include "Ebola Beat Our Land", "In the Cold", "A Cry of a Mother" and many more.

9. **Kainwo, JEM**, whose real name is Jeelo Kainwo, was born in Freetown, Sierra Leone. She is married to Henry Olayemi Kallon & the daughter of Rev. Moses & Rev Mrs. Violet Kainwo. Although she has never had a formal training in the poetic art, she has been writing since she was 7 (seven) years old; having been introduced to it by her dad. One of her poems 'Permutations' was published in the Sierra Leonean anthology "Kalashnikov in the Sun" published by Pika Press in 2006. She is also a Barrister & Solicitor-at-law called to the Sierra Leonean Bar in 2010 & a holder of an LLM in International Criminal Law from the National University of Ireland, Galway. Jeelo loves to sing, cook and watch videos on YouTube when she is not otherwise engaged in poetry or the law.

10. **Kamara, Fatmata Lilian** was born and raised as the first child of her parents in the eastern part of Freetown. She went to the St. Joseph Primary and Secondary Schools and she holds a diploma in Business Administration at the Milton Margai College of education and currently reading for a BSc. in Social Work at the Fourah Bay College, University of Sierra Leone. She has so much fascination for the Arts.

11. **Kamara, Joseph Sherman** was born in the city of Bo, Southern Sierra Leone. He moved to Freetown at preschool age in the early eighties and spent his entire childhood in Kissy, in the eastern suburbs of Freetown, where he attended the Kankaylay Islamic Primary School and later the Methodist Boys' High School. His interest and skills in poetry were nurtured at the Methodist Boys' High School through a curriculum that compelled science students to learn literature under the tutelage of some of the best literature teachers in the country at that time. However, the seeds of poetry planted in him during those tender years have remained dormant over the year, being suppressed by limited professional demand for flowery language in a teaching and research career in Agricultural

Engineering at Njala University, Sierra Leone. It seems the recent circumstances around him have provided the right timing and fertility for these seeds to flourish. Joseph is a hobby poet at the moment, but believes that poetry and creative writing in general will become more important to him in the coming years as his desire to share his thoughts, emotions and experiences get stronger with age.

12. **Kamarah, Sheikh Umarr (Prof.)** is a Sierra Leonean Professor of English and Linguistics at Virginia State University in the United States of America. He is currently the Chair of the Department of Languages and Literature at Virginia State University. He earned an HTC from Milton Margai Teachers College, now Milton Margai College of Education and Technology, a B.A. (Hons) in English from Fourah Bay College, an M.A. in Linguistics from the University of Leeds, and a Ph.D. in Linguistics from the University of Wisconsin at Madison. Sheikh Umarr Kamarah has served as Lecturer at Fourah Bay College (USL), and University of Wisconsin at Madison; Assistant Professor at Shaw University, and Professor at Virginia State University in the United States of America. He was a Fulbright Specialist in Applied Linguistics in 2011. He has published three volumes of poetry---*The Child of War* (2000), *Singing in Exile* (2002), and *An Anthology of Krio Poetry*. He has also published

A Descriptive Grammar of KʌThemnɛ (2007). He has published several book chapters and peer reviewed articles. Professor Kamarah is a Consultant on Language Analysis for the Federal Department of Immigration, Switzerland and for De Taalstudio, a language analysis institution in Amsterdam, Netherlands. He is an External Examiner in Linguistics, University of Sierra Leone. He is a member of numerous professional organizations including Linguistic Society of America, Association of Forensic Linguists, International Language and Law Association and African Literature Association. He also serves as a member on the editorial board of the Africana Bulletin, Journal of the University of Sierra Leone and on the editorial board of the Sierra Leone Writers Series (for Literature and Linguistics).

13. **Kargbo, Brian Sitta** is a poet and a versatile writer (Short Story writer, Speechwriter, Songwriter and playwright). He is currently working on his first book—an anthology of fifty poems. For nine years, Brian has been a dedicated advocate for children and youth in

204

Sierra Leone and has been actively involved in Girl Child campaigns. On different occasions, he has been recognized and rewarded for his contributions—best head boy of his school in 2003 (awarded by the *Anti- Violence Movement*) at the Sierra Leone Grammar School (SLGS) completing his secondary education at the Prince of Wales where he served as president of *the Literary and Debating Society* (L&DS). He is presently the Coordinator of the Sierra Leone Broadcasting Corporation (SLBC) *Voice of Children Project* (VOC), Adviser for *Children Broadcasters Network* (CBN) and a member of *Sierra Leone Youth Coalition on HIV/AIDS* (SLYCHA); the *Oracle Book Club* and *Young Writers of Sierra Leone*. Whiles in school, he established the *Children in Action for Attitudinal Change* (CAFAC). He is currently a student of Fourah Bay College (FBC), University of Sierra Leone.

14. **Konteh, Iyerich Bomkapr Eva** is a student pursuing a BSc (Hons) degree in Public Health at the University of Anglia Ruskin in Cambridge, United Kingdom.

15. **Mansaray, Khadi** is a writer, publisher and activist. She is the founder of *Sondiata Global Media*, a publishing house for the African Diaspora; *Books Not Babies Project*, which helps pregnant teenagers get an education and *Nefertiti Reborn*, a women's leadership blog. She is also an accountant and Project Manager. She used to work for RBS Insurance and Direct Line Group.

16. **Sankoh, Osman Alimamy (Prof.)**, known to most Sierra Leoneans as **Mallam O.**, was born in Warima in Sierra Leone. He attended Tomlinson High School, Songo. He obtained a BSc Ed. (Mathematics) degree with distinction from Njala University, Sierra Leone. He further holds the following degrees: BSc Hons. (Statistics); MSc (Applied Statistics); and DSc (Applied Statistics) from the Technical University of Dortmund, Germany. He is currently the Executive Director of the INDEPTH Network, a health information international NGO located in Accra, Ghana, where he lives with his family. Mallam O. established the Sierra Leonean Writers Series (SLWS) in 2001 and, as his own contribution to nation building, now publishes books by writers of Sierra Leonean origin.

17. **Sesay, Oumar Farouk** became known in Sierra Leone literary scene when he was resident playwright of Bai Bureh Theatre in the '80s. Several of his plays were performed in the then City hall and

he won accolades among his peers. He veered into journalism and wrote for several local and international newspapers. He has been published in many anthologies of Sierra Leonean poets, including *Lice in the Lion's Mane*, *Songs That Pour the Heart* and *Kalashnikov in the Sun*. AFRIKA IM GEDICHT. He has also written short stories; *The Price*, published by Sierra Leone writers Series and *Closure* published by Sierra Arts publishers. His first volume of poems, Salute to the Remains of a Peasant was published in 2007 in America. *The Edge of a Cry* is his second collection of poems. He has also written his first novel; *Landscape of Memories* published by SLWS. He was Cadbury Visiting Fellow in 2009 at the Centre for West African Studies in the University of Birmingham. He has participated in several poetry festivals and workshop in Sierra Leone, UK, Colombia, United States and Hong Kong. His poems have been translated into German and Spanish. He is a graduate of Fourah Bay College, University of Sierra Leone.

18. **Sheriff, Mohamed** writes children stories, short stories, novellas and drama for radio TV and stage. He produces and directs documentary videos, short films, radio, TV and stage plays for both entertainment and social change projects. He has won several local and international awards for his productions and writings including Best Short Film, "Victims", We Own TV National Film Festival 2012, Best Docudrama Film, "Sombodi Ep Mi", Sierra International Film Festival 2 (SLIFF2) 2013 and three BBC playwriting and many short story awards (Just Me and Mama, Spots of a Leopard, and A Voice in Hell) and the ECOWAS Prize for Excellence in Literature for "Secret Fear", a novella for teenagers, published by Macmillan Publishers.

19. **Taqi, Fatou** nee Cole is a mother of three and president of the 50/50 Group in Sierra Leone. She works at the University of Sierra Leone as a lecturer in the Language Studies Department & the Institute for Gender Research & Documentation, Fourah Bay College and she is also the director of the Academic & Career Advisory & Counselling Services. She holds a PhD in Social Sciences and is very passionate about gender equity and gender empowerment. She enjoys travelling, the arts and networking.

20. **Taylor, James Bernard** works in Project Management after graduate studies at the University of Maryland (UMUC), USA. Prior to that, Taylor worked for the US Department of State for twenty-

three years as Director, Information Resource Centre at the US Embassy in Freetown. He also taught at the Methodist Girls High School and the Institute of Public Administration and Management (IPAM), University of Sierra Leone (Social Work Program). He is a published writer and poet with some of his works found in *Songs that Pour the Heart: Poems from Sierra Leone; Leoneanthology: Contemporary short stories and poems from Sierra Leone, and The Price and Other Stories.* He has also written many non-fictional pieces on socio-political issues in several newspapers. In addition to writing, Taylor has a passion for classical music and photography. He plays musical instruments which includes the piano/organ, accordion, guitar and euphonium and has composed classical and gospel music for choral performances.

21. **Thompson, Celia** is a journalist and media practitioner. She currently co-hosts the 'Day Break West Africa' breakfast show on West Africa Democracy radio in Dakar, Senegal. Lived and worked in Sudan and South Sudan, respectively, between 2007 and 2014; served as a Peacekeeper for the UN Peace Keeping missions (UNMIS & UNMISS) and then as Programs Head (Radio Miraya)—Foundation Hirondelle—a Swiss Non-governmental media outfit. Prior to that, Ms Thompson worked for the UN Mission in Sierra Leone during the post-conflict era-- facilitating the Voice of Children project, with over 200 children including ex-combatants and war orphans. She holds a Bachelor in Arts degree with Honours in Linguistics, together with International diplomas in Advertising, Media Studies and Modern Management, from the Cambridge International College. Ms Thompson is a Rotarian.

22. **Thompson, Pelham Jonathan Adeleke** was born on 21st December, 1985. He holds a diploma in Peace and Conflict Studies from Fourah Bay College (USL) and is currently reading for a degree in Mass Communication at the University of Makeni (UNIMAK). He has written plays such as "No Recoil", "Dance Ibidumi Dance", "Dance in the Garden", "Lady Leone" and is now working on his first novel, "Bitter Leaves".

23. **Thulla, Philip Foday Yamba** was born in Lunar, Sierra Leone. He holds a master's degree from Njala University in Sierra Leone. He has published a compilation of short stories, *Homecoming: Knowing My*

People and Other Stories and co-authored a short novel entitled *The Chameleon Goes Home.* He is presently a PhD candidate in African Folk literature (The Temne People) and a lecturer in Literature in the Institute of Languages and Cultural Studies, Njala University, Sierra Leone. He has just completed a full-length fictional memoir entitled, *Saving the State House: the Confession of a Thug.*

24. **Wilson, Randoulph L.A**. is a poet, writer, actor and broadcaster. He earned a Bachelor of Arts Degree at the Fourah Bay Collage, University of Sierra Leone and a master's degree in Public Administration from the Njala University. He was an English Language and Literature in English tutor at his alma mater, the Albert Academy (UMC). He is currently a part-time lecturer in English Language at the Institute of Public Administration and Management (IPAM).

25. **Yawmah, Jusu Jaka** studied at the College of Medicine and Allied Health Sciences, University of Sierra Leone for an MBChB after completing his secondary school education at the Prince of Wales, Kingtom in Freetown. Back then, his friends named him "Yawma, the poet" because of his avid interest in poetry. He was the best Literature student among his Senior Secondary School peers though he was a science student.

SIERRA LEONEAN WRITERS SERIES (SLWS)

Focusing on academic, fictional, and scientific writing that will complement other relevant materials used in schools, colleges, universities and other tertiary institutions, the Sierra Leonean Writers Series (SLWS) aims to promote good quality books by Sierra Leoneans writing on any topics and other writers from around the world who write on themes and issues about Sierra Leone.

It is the publisher's hope that students and other readers in Sierra Leone will eventually be at least some of the primary beneficiaries of these works. Not only will people in Sierra Leone be able to read materials that relate to their own lives and experiences, budding writers will also be able to draw inspiration from the efforts of their compatriots and other established writers.

Submitted work undergoes a rigorous peer-review process before being accepted for publication, with an international editorial board providing guidance to writers.

SLWS, based in Warima and Freetown in Sierra Leone, distributes books globally through AMAZON.COM. In Sierra Leone, SLWS books are currently available at the SLWS Bookshop in Warima (near Masiaka) and at CLC Bookshop, 92 Pademba Road in Freetown.

SLWS co-publishes some titles with Karantha Publishers in Sierra Leone.

For further information, please visit our website: www.sl-writers-series.org
or contact the publisher, Prof. Osman A. Sankoh (Mallam O.) publisher@sl-writers-series.org

Published Books – a milestone of the 50th title has been reached in September 2016!

1	Osman A. Sankoh (Mallam O.)	2001/ 2016	*A Memoir*	*Hybrid Eyes – An African in Europe*
2	Osman A. Sankoh (Mallam O.)	2001	*Non-fiction*	*Beautiful Colours*
3	Sheikh Umarr	2002/ 2015	*Poems*	*Singing in Exile and The*

	Kamarah			*Child of War*
4	Abdul B. Kamara	2003/ 2015	*A Memoir*	*Unknown Destination*
5	Samuel Hinton	2003	*Poems*	*The Road to Kenema*
6	Karamoh Kabba	2005/ 2016	*A Novel*	*Morquee – The Political Drama of Wish over Wisdom*
7	Yema Lucilda Hunter	2007	*A Novel*	*Redemption Song*
8	Joe A. D. Alie	2007/ 2015	*Research Text*	*Sierra Leone Since Independence – History of a Postcolonial State*
9	Mohamed Combo Kamanda	2007	*A Play*	*The Visa*
10	J Sorie Conteh	2007	*A Novel*	*In Search of Sons*
11	Michael Fayia Kallon	2010/ 2015	*A Novel*	*The Ghosts of Ngaingah*
12	J Sorie Conteh	2011	*A Novel*	*Family Affairs*
13	Winston Forde	2011	*A Play*	*Layila, Kakatua wan bi Lida*

14	Eustace Palmer Doc P.	2012	*A Novel*	*A Pillar of the Community*
15	Siaka Kroma	2012	*Non-fiction*	*Manners Maketh Man – Adventures of a Bo School Boy*
16	Mohamed Combo Kamanda (ed)	2012	*Short Stories*	*The Price and other Short Stories from Sierra Leone*
17	Sigismond Tucker	2013	*A Memoir*	*From the Land of Diamonds to the Isle of Spice*
18	Bailah Leigh	2013	*Non-fiction*	*Dilemma of Freedom – A Diary from Behind Rebels Lines in the Sierra Leone Civil War*
19	Nnamdi Carew	2013	*A Novella*	*Tiger Fist – Two Stories*
20	Yema Lucilda Hunter	2013	*A Novel*	*Joy Came in the Morning*
21	Ebenezer 'Solo' Collier	2013	*Resear ch Text*	*Primary & Secondary Education in Sierra Leone – Evaluation of more than 50 years of*

				PRACTICES & POLICIES
22	Gbananom Hallowell	2013	*Short Stories*	*Gbomgbosoro - Two Stories*
23	Sheikh Umarr Kamarah & Majorie Jones (eds)	2013	*Poems*	*beg sol noba kuk sup - An Anthology of Krio Poetry*
24	Siaka Kroma	2014	*Short Stories*	*Tales from the Fireside*
25	Syl Cheney-Coker**	2014	*Poems*	*The Road to Jamaica*
26	Dr Sama Banya	2015	*A Memoir*	*Looking Back – My Life and Times*
27	Andrew K Keili	2015	*Social Commentary*	*Ponder My Thoughts – Vol. 1*
28	Jedidah A. O. Johnson	2015	*A Novel*	*Youthful Yearnings*
29	Oumar Farouk Sesay	2015	*A Novel*	*Landscape of Memories*
30	Oumar Farouk Sesay	2015	*Poems*	*The Edge of a Cry*
31	Gbanabom Hallowell	2015	*A Novel*	*The Road to Kaibara*

32	Mohamed Gibril Sesay*	2015	*A Novel*	*This Side of Nothingness*
33	Yema Lucilda Hunter	2015	*A Novel*	*Nanna*
34	Yusuf Bangura	2015	*Research Text*	*Development, Democracy & Cohesion*
35	Lansana Gberie	2015	*Research Text*	*War, Politics & Justice in West Africa*
36	Yema Lucilda Hunter	2015	*A Biography*	*An African Treasure: In Search of Gladys Casely-Hayford 1904-1950*
37	Moses Kainwo	2015	*Poems*	*Ayo Ayo Ayo and other Love Songs*
38	Abdulai Walon-Jalloh	2015	*Poems*	*Voices and Passions*
39	Gbanabom Hallowell (Ed.)	2016	*Short Stories*	*In the Belly of the Lion – An Anthology of new Sierra Leonean Short Stories*
40	Ahmed Koroma	2016	*Poems*	*Along the Odokoko River - Poems*

41	George Coleridge-Taylor	2016	*A Memoir*	*Transformation in Transition*
42	Karamoh Kabba	2016	*Research Text*	*Fire from Timbuktu: A Dialogue with History*
43	Umu Kultumie Tejan-Jalloh	2016	*A Memoir*	*Telling It As It Was: The Career of A Sierra Leonean Woman in Public Service*
44	Ambrose Massaquoi	2016	*Poems*	*Along the Peal of Drums: Collected Poems (1990-2015)*
45	Mohamed Gibril Sesay	2016	*Poems*	*At the Gathering of Roads (Poems)*
46	Gbanabom Hallowell	2016	*Poems*	*Manscape in the Sierra: New and Collected Poems 1991-2011*
47	Gbanabom Hallowell (Ed.)	2016	*Short Stories and Poems*	*Leoneanthology: Comtemporary Short Stories and Poems from Sierra Leone*

48	Gbanabom Hallowell	2016	*Poems*	*Don't Call Me Elvis and Other Poems*
49	Bakar Mansaray	2016	*Short Stories*	*A Suitcase Full of Dried Fish and Other Stories*
50	Gbanabom Hallowell	2016	*Poems*	*The Art of the Lonely Wanderer*

*co-published with Karantha Publishers

www.ingramcontent.com/pod-product-compliance
Lightning Source LLC
Chambersburg PA
CBHW031835090426
42741CB00005B/251